Report

Valuing Women:
Making Women Visible

Dr Kathryn Hodges and Dr Sarah Burch
Foreword by Chine McDonald

Contents

This report in 30 seconds	5
Acknowledgements	7
Foreword	9
Executive Summary	12
Introduction	20
Part One: What We Already Know	31
Intersecting lived experiences: The things that happen to women	32
Helping services: Understanding why women attend, leave and return	43
Shaped by faith: Faith-based social care provision	49
Part Two: Finding Out More	60
To trust and be trusted	61
Valuing women	71
Prayer: A gift, reflection, and unity	79
Resources: tensions and opportunities	86
Conclusion	95
Recommendations	102

This report in 30 seconds

Some women experience severe and multiple disadvantage within their lives. This disadvantage includes abuse and trauma, mental ill-health, homelessness, isolation, poverty, and sexual exploitation. These experiences, and the women who live through them, commonly go unrecognised. Similarly, there are sizeable gaps in terms of the support available.

These gaps can be found either in a failure to provide support, or to provide support in a way that is useful or safe for women. When women are unable to access effective, trustworthy, and reliable helping services, there can be fatal consequences. Effective help for women needs to understand the impact of the things that happen to women, provide continuity of care, and build trusting, respectful relationships.

This study offers a snapshot of the experiences of staff and volunteers, from six Christian faith-based organisations, who support women. They drew on their faith and the resources of their organisations, committing to a continuity of care, which fostered trust. They valued the women they worked with and described their work as a privilege. A number commented that they met women in the image of God, as equals with whom it was a privilege to work. For many their faith was a source of strength and comfort, in which prayer could be offered as a gift, provided an opportunity to reflect on their work, or was experienced as a source of unity.

The level of care which was shown to women is not unique to the faith-based sector. But the staff and volunteers in this study took a distinctive approach which made the women they worked with truly visible through their regard. This study makes the work of the staff and volunteers visible in turn.

Acknowledgements

Authors' Acknowledgements

We are hugely grateful to the staff and volunteers who gave their time to be involved in this research. Our thanks are extended to: Amber Chaplains, Caritas Bakhita House, Eve, Faith House (Salvation Army), Lighthouse, and Youth with a Mission.

We would like to thank Porticus for funding this research and Theos for their support of this project. Particular thanks are due to Theos colleagues, Dr Madeleine Pennington, Dr Nick Spencer, Lizzie Harvey and Chine McDonald, who commented on drafts of this report. We are very grateful to Dr Madeleine Pennington who provided additional text and clarity to the report. Thanks also to Ben Ryan who invited a research proposal on this subject and sought funding.

A small advisory group supported the work of this project, and we are very grateful for thoughtful input from Dr Sophie Cartwright and Dr Lyndsey Harris. Thanks to Rev. Dr Philip Howlett who provided comment on a section of this report.

Theos Acknowledgements

Theos is extremely grateful to the authors for their work in completing this research, and especially their tenacity in adapting the research to the limitations inevitably imposed by the pandemic.

We also want to thank the funders of the project, Porticus, without whose generous support the work would simply not have been possible.

Foreword

International Women's Day this year asks us to imagine a gender equal world, free from stereotypes and discrimination and calls on us to collectively break the bias against women. Women all over the world face barriers, many of them suffering from extreme and intersecting inequalities including poverty and sexual violence, and barriers to progress.

But closer to home, there exists a group of women often unseen, who face severe and multiple disadvantage, and who are being failed by a range of systems in the UK unable to holistically support women. Issues they face include abuse, mental ill-health, homelessness, trauma and sexual exploitation.

Theos exists to enrich the conversation about the role of faith in society, including demonstrating how people motivated by their faith contribute to flourishing communities. Our 'Doing Good' stream explores faith-based social action; and it is into this context that we publish this report, researched by social worker and academic Dr Kathryn Hodges, and co-authored by Dr Kathryn Hodges and academic Dr Sarah Burch.

Valuing Women: Making Women Visible brings into sharp focus the lives of those women experiencing severe and multiple disadvantage – women who are often overlooked, lost in a system creaking at the seams following years of austerity.

This research draws attention to the important role Christian organisations in the social care sector can play in tackling the disadvantage women face, and the structures that prevent them from being truly seen and helped.

The report explores the ways in which Christian organisations – though not without their own challenges

– are extremely well placed to make visible the women they work with. Internally, their faith motivations and theological understanding of the value of every human being as made in God's image encourage them to treat the women as of equal worth and in no way less deserving of stability, care and love. Externally, Christian organisations are supported by their faith community who can act as added resource, including through raising much-needed funds for specific purposes, and enable the organisations to have a level of independence that helps them navigate the systems that are increasingly not fit for purpose.

We hope this report will go some way towards a better understanding of the complex challenges faced by some of the most disadvantaged women in our society, draw attention to the changes that are needed in supporting women, and demonstrate how the wisdom, experience and practice of Christian organisations might help to meet some of these challenges.

Chine McDonald
Director, Theos

Executive Summary

Background

There is a continued failure to understand the intersecting lived experiences of women experiencing severe and multiple disadvantage.[1] This ongoing ignorance leaves women not only experiencing harm and abuse, but also means that when they seek help there are sizeable gaps in terms of the support available.

These gaps can be found either in a failure to provide support, or to provide support in a way that is useful or safe for women. When women are unable to access effective, trustworthy, and reliable helping services, there can be fatal consequences.

Community social care services are under strain. Not only have they faced ongoing and drastic cuts following the financial crisis (and are likely to face further cuts in the wake of the COVID-19 pandemic), but for third sector services this financial strain has been accompanied by greater regulation in response to the increasingly bureaucratic demands of local authority funders. As women are higher users of welfare provision than men, they are disproportionately affected by cuts to services or benefits.

Ten years of austerity, accompanied by these heavier administrative burdens, have created further restrictions and limitations on the available support for women experiencing multiple and severe disadvantage.

Where services are funded mostly or entirely by non-governmental bodies (e.g. through charitable giving, philanthropy, or religious groups), organisations have greater levels of autonomy in the way they provide support. This enables helping services to provide care in a way that is valuable to women. For some women this will be lifesaving.

This research explores not only whether Christian charities are filling a gap in welfare provision for women, but also considers how this support is provided and experienced, and what can be learnt from it. This in-depth study, undertaken during 2020-2021, heard from 21 staff and volunteers at six Christian charities supporting women experiencing multiple and severe disadvantage.

The study is a snapshot of the way staff and volunteers talk about their experiences of providing support to women at a Christian charity. It is not comparing faith-based organisations (FBO) and secular care provision, and the findings should be read in this context.

Findings

Four clear themes emerged from the interviews: the trusting relationships needed to support women experiencing multiple and severe disadvantage; the way the faith and values of staff and volunteers affected the way they met women; the utilisation of prayer by some in their work; and the tensions and opportunities found in resourcing helping services.

To trust and be trusted

Trusting relationships are needed to support women who have histories of trauma, and are key when creating safe environments. Women's experiences of abuse and deprivation are often compounded by inadequate responses from services. Staff and volunteers talked of many women who had been seen as 'too complex' for existing services, rendered invisible by a lack of recognition of their situations and left dealing with isolation, mental ill-health and a range of other intersecting disadvantages. These experiences eroded women's capacity to trust. Staff and volunteers prioritised developing relationships and understood the barriers women faced when trusting support services to help.

Valuing women

Beliefs and values of staff and volunteers informed how they met and provided support to women. Staff and volunteers talked about how they saw women they supported "in the image of God", as equals with whom it was a privilege to work. This moved them away from the potential power imbalance that can arise in the practitioner/client relationship, particularly when working with individuals who may have experienced stigma. Not all staff were of faith, but those who were spoke of the way it helped them value women and see them as more than a series of problems to be fixed. They drew on the idea of going the extra mile, as taken from scripture, to inform their care.

Prayer: A gift, reflection, and unity

There was frequent mention of prayer throughout the interviews. Although not everyone prayed, or prayed in the same way, those that did found it a source of strength in many ways. Prayer was offered as a gift to the women that staff and volunteers supported, a way of showing them that their lives were witnessed and that they were loved. Prayer also gave staff and volunteers a place and time to pause and reflect on their work, and a way to connect to others.

Resources: tensions and opportunities

The way organisations drew on their resources was explored. Often, they were taking creative or longer-term approaches by filling the gaps left by statutory services. Organisations were able to rely on a degree of independent funding from their wider faith communities, which gave an element of freedom and security and supported continuity of care. Yet there were also tensions which left staff and volunteers torn between supporting individual women or campaigning for wider change to provision.

Conclusion

Key messages that emerged from this study brought attention to the invisibility of women, the application of faith in social care practice, and how there is much to be learnt from the way Christian charities value and meet women.

Broadly faith-based organisations prefer to provide unconditional as well as longer term support, which is arguably more helpful to women experiencing multiple and severe disadvantage. The focus on relational and unconditional practice, sometimes without detailed knowledge of the 'problem' or the outcomes they were seeking to achieve, enables the flexibility to provide support in a way that is responsive to women.

Visibility

The work of the charities involved was largely invisible. This reflects how women helped by this work are frequently rendered invisible by wider society. The experiences and knowledge of the staff working at these faith-based organisations should be heard. There is much to be learnt in what they have witnessed, and there are many obvious ideas for system change that would significantly benefit the women they support.

Faith in practice

Many of the staff and volunteers brought faith to their work in distinctive ways, and it underpinned how they met women and provided support. Faith was infused into practice.

Faith was part of the motivation of staff and volunteers, providing support to women in often very difficult circumstances. Faith enabled them to experience a sense of unity within their organisations and to work with women from a position of equal value.

Meeting women, valuing women

The preference of faith-based organisations for a relational approach to practice enables them to meet women with detailed knowledge and understanding of their intersecting lived experiences and the barriers to seeking help and support. They work to ensure that they can create environments of trust and safety for women seeking help and support.

Christian charities are part of a bigger network and community of support and are well placed to bring attention to the injustice experienced by women, the care needed, and the care provided.

Recommendations

— Christian charities need to be recognised and valued locally and nationally for their work in the community, no matter the size or perceived impact of their provision.

— There is much talk about the value of relational and trauma-informed approaches to care, but the application to practice is harder. There is much to be learnt here from the way the Christian charities involved in this study provided support.

— Services and staff need support in challenging the bad practice, unhelpful service provision, and/or oppressive systems that they witness.

- Safe, secure, and supported housing for women is a priority. There seems to be an opportunity here for faith-based organisations to bring their unconditional approaches to care, long-term relationships, and alternative funding and resourcing, to consider how they can develop effective residential support for women.
- Elements of this research that would benefit from being explored further.
    - There is limited research exploring women and FBOs, in terms of those receiving and providing care, and this should be remedied given the likely proportion of women in both groups.
    - It would also be useful to investigate further the threads of connecting reflective practice and prayer in care provision, and the impact of 'going the extra mile' on staff and volunteers.
    - The situation for women experiencing severe and multiple disadvantage is complex. This needs to be witnessed and action taken to challenge the ongoing failure to adequately respond and support women. Staff and volunteers would benefit from support when taking social action (at the micro, meso or macro level), or in deciding not to take it, as they balance the tensions of supporting women whilst fighting for justice.

[1] 'Severe and multiple disadvantage' explains the things that happen to people because of society's actions, rather than a person's own choices. See p. 34 below for a fuller description.

Introduction

Introduction

Community social care services are under strain. Not only have they faced ongoing and drastic cuts following the financial crisis (and are likely to face further cuts in the wake of the COVID-19 pandemic), but for third sector services this financial strain has been accompanied by greater regulation in response to the increasingly bureaucratic demands of local authority funders.[1] As women are higher users of welfare provision than men, they are disproportionately affected by cuts to services or benefits.[2]

Local authority spending power has fallen by 18% since 2010, and there are knock-on effects – one of which is the £7 million cut in council funding to domestic violence refuges between 2010 and 2018.[3]

This combination of a heavier administrative burden and fewer resources to cope with it has had a profound effect on service provision for women and the way helping services respond to those who seek their support.[4]

Many of the issues women and girls face are highly gendered and are associated with severe disadvantage. Women make up 83.5% of victims of domestic violence and abuse, whilst men are the defendants in the majority of domestic abuse cases (92.1%).[5] Victims of sexual exploitation are predominantly women exploited by male buyers and pimps.[6] Evidence gathered in the UK and globally shows the sex industry "as a context in which sexual and physical violence, perpetrated by men against women and

> **Local authority spending power has fallen by 18% since 2010, including a £7 million cut in council funding to domestic violence refuges from 2010-18.**

girls, is pervasive."[7] It is mainly women who sell sex or exchange sex for other goods or services that they need (such as rent, drugs and so on), and men who are the buyers and pimps.[8] The demand for buying sex informs supply, and women are trafficked by organised crime networks who exploit this demand.[9]

Restrictions on what support third sector providers can offer women frequently stem from expectations set as part of commissioning processes, often in response to national policy directives.[10] These restrictions, alongside diminishing funding, have transformed the landscape of third sector women's services in recent years, leading some organisations to close and others to merge.[11] Without third sector women's services, there has been a greater reliance on statutory provision,[12] and these are key services that are also struggling and unable to provide much beyond their basic statutory duties.[13]

There are many services funded mostly or in their entirety by non-governmental bodies, either from charitable giving, philanthropy, or religious groups.

As a result, there has been steadily increasing demand for the decimated specialist third sector women's services.[14] A vicious circle has been created, within which "women are paying the price".[15]

There are many services funded mostly or in their entirety by non-governmental bodies, either from charitable giving, philanthropy, or religious groups, meaning the resources they rely on are not restricted by governmental policy. This gives organisations greater levels of creativity and autonomy.[16] In a challenging community landscape, this allows helping services to provide support in a way that is valuable, and even lifesaving, to women.

This study

This in-depth study explores the way that Christian charities provide support to women experiencing multiple and severe disadvantage. It will not just establish whether Christian charities are filling a gap in welfare provision, but consider *how* this support is provided and experienced, and what can be learnt from it.

The following research questions underpinned this study:

— In what ways do Christian charities explain the support they offer to women experiencing multiple and severe disadvantage?

— What are staff and volunteers' experiences of providing help and support to women?

— How are the values of faith-based organisations evident in the way volunteers and staff support women?

— What can be learnt about (and from) the ways Christian charities provide support to women?

The first part of this report establishes the context of this research. It summarises the wider literature about the intersecting lived experiences of women – the things that happen to women. It also gives an overview of what is known about the way women experience helping services, clarifying the importance that should be given to the way women are met and heard when seeking support. Part one concludes with a brief overview of faith-based social care provision, and briefly outlines the way faith-based organisations (FBOs) tend to provide unconditional support, and how this is helpful to women experiencing multiple and severe disadvantage.

Part two of the report sets out the four themes that emerged from the interviews with staff and volunteers at six Christian charities. This study is a snapshot of the way the staff and volunteers talk about their experiences of providing support to women at a Christian charity. It is not comparing FBO and secular care provision, and the findings should be read in this context.

The first theme, to trust and be trusted, explores how trusting relationships are needed to support women who have histories of trauma, and the priority of creating safe environments.

Valuing women illustrates the way beliefs and values of staff and volunteers informed how they met and provided support to women. Staff and volunteers talked about how they saw women they supported in the image of God, as equals, with whom it was a privilege to work. This moved them away from the potential power imbalance that can arise in the practitioner/client relationship, particularly when supporting individuals who are commonly stigmatised.

Prayer: A gift, reflection, and unity examines the frequent mention of prayer throughout the interviews. There is discussion about the way it can be offered as a gift to the women staff and volunteers support, as a place and time to pause and reflect on their work, and a way to connect to others.

The final theme, *Resources: tensions and opportunities*, explores the ways in which organisations drew on their resources, often by taking creative or longer-term approaches, to fill the gaps left by statutory services. However, there were also tensions which left staff and volunteers torn between either supporting individual women or campaigning for wider change to provision.

The key messages of this study are set out in the conclusion. Attention is brought to the invisibility of the charities and the women that they help; the way many staff and volunteers infuse their faith into practice and its impact on how they meet and support women; and how the application of relational approaches leads women to be valued and met in a way that is more helpful to them, underpinned by a detailed knowledge of lived experiences and the barriers to accessing support.

Recommendations focus on: the need for greater recognition and value of the work of Christian charities in supporting women; that services and staff should be supported in challenging unhelpful practice and oppressive systems they witness in the course of their work; and how support should be made available to those services that decide to take social action at a micro, meso or macro level.

There is much to be learnt from the way Christian charities involved in this study provided support, in particular their relational approach to care. The recommendations highlight the opportunity for FBOs to bring their resources and approaches to care to provide safe, secure, and supported housing for women. In addition, elements of this research would benefit from further exploration, including: women and FBOs; prayer and reflective practice in care provision; and the impact of 'going the extra mile' on staff and volunteers.

Research methodology

This is an in-depth qualitative study, in which semi-structured interviews were used to hear the experiences of 21 staff and volunteers (all female) who worked at six Christian charities supporting women experiencing "multiple and severe disadvantage" (see p. 34 for a fuller description of this term).

Broadly the charities were providing support to women involved in prostitution, those who had been trafficked, and victims, survivors and perpetrators of domestic violence and abuse (DVA). All the organisations were based in England apart from one project delivering services in Amsterdam as part of the charity's international work. Of the charities based in England, three were based in London, one in a large Midlands town, and one in a city in the North-East.

Charities provided support to women through outreach;[17] drop-in appointments at a centre; group activities; one-to-one support and advocacy; group structured recovery programmes; and through residential care at a safehouse.

Organisations were identified as Christian FBOs, using the frame of reference established by researchers exploring FBOs and support provided to victims and survivors of modern slavery.[18] Here it has been amended to replace the terms faith and religion with 'Christian'. Therefore, this study identified Christian FBOs by examining the presence of: "explicit or implicit Christian references in the mission statement and other documents; any links to a specific Christian institution (e.g. a church); whether profiles of trustees and staff stated their Christian faith or membership of a Christian body; and any requirements for Christian affiliation in job advertisements."

Staff and volunteers were asked four broad questions about the journey to their current role and what they do, the experience of providing help and support to others, and the way they understood faith-based values informing their work. The questions were kept to a minimum, so as not to limit participants' narratives. The role of the social researcher is to encourage participants to reflect on their everyday experiences, so that they can understand the world as seen by individuals and the meanings they apply to it.[19]

Ethical approval was granted by St. Mary's University Ethics Sub-Committee and the Salvation Army Research and Development Service. Interviews were carried out via video calls between November 2020 and September 2021. Written consent was sought from participants at the beginning of each interview, and all were audio recorded and later transcribed. These transcriptions were coded and thematically analysed using NVivo software.

Interviewees were asked to provide another name so they could recognise themselves in the research whilst remaining anonymous. We have further maintained this anonymity by not linking organisations to interviewees in this report, and changing the names of places.

A note on the impact of COVID-19

When this research project was initially conceived, we intended to talk to women who received support from the Christian charities involved in the research. We wanted to hear from women about the ways they experienced helping services, what they noticed about faith-based provision, and what was helpful or otherwise.

However, the first COVID-19 lockdown began in parallel with the start of the research, making it impossible to carry out face-to-face interviews with women who accessed the Christian charities for reasons of their own safety and broader ethical concerns. We refocused the project to hear from staff and volunteers only. Additionally, during this time many helping services had to adjust the way they provided support; a little of this experience has been heard in the interviews.

To ensure women's voices are at the heart of this report, and to provide context for the interviews with support staff and volunteers, quotes from two previous studies have been interwoven with the text of Part One.[20] The first explored the decisions and choices women experiencing multiple and severe disadvantage make when seeking help and support, and heard from 11 women attending a faith-based service in an English city.[21] The second study heard from 114 women located across England, about their experiences of exiting prostitution and the available support.[22] Women are identified by their name or as a study participant, and so forth, depending on how they were represented in the research.

1 Molly Warrington, 'Fleeing from fear: The changing role of refuges in meeting the needs of women leaving violent partners', *Capital & Class* Vol 27, No. 2 (1 July 2003): pp 123–50, *doi.org/10.1177/030981680308000108*

2 Fran Bennett, 'Women and "Welfare Reform" in the UK', *Asia and the Pacific Society Policy Forum*, 2019. *www.policyforum.net/women-and-welfare-reform-in-the-uk/*

3 Institute for Government, 'Local Government Funding in England', The Institute for Government, 10 March 2020. *www.instituteforgovernment.org.uk/explainers/local-government-funding-england*; Jamie Grierson, 'Council Funding for Women's Refuges Cut by Nearly £7m since 2010', *The Guardian*, 23 March 2018. *www.theguardian.com/society/2018/mar/23/council-funding-womens-refuges-cut-since-2010-england-wales-scotland*

4 Grierson, 'Council Funding for Women's Refuges Cut by Nearly £7m since 2010'; Warrington, 'Fleeing from Fear'.

5 Crown Prosecution Service, 'Violence against Women and Girls Report 2017-18' (Crown Prosecution Service, 2018). PDF available at: *www.cps.gov.uk/sites/default/files/documents/publications/cps-vawg-report-2018.pdf*

6 Maddy Coy, 'Introduction: Prostitution, Harm and Gender Inequality', in Maddy Coy (Ed), *Prostitution, Harm and Gender Inequality: Theory, Research and Policy*, (Abingdon, Oxon: Routledge, 2016), pp. 1-12.

7 Maddy Coy, 'Joining the dots on sexual exploitation of children and women: A way forward for UK policy responses', Critical Social Policy Vol 36, No. 4 (April2016): pp. 578. *doi.org/10.1177/0261018316638460*

8 Coy, 'Introduction: Prostitution, Harm and Gender Inequality...'; Monica O'Connor, *The Sex Economy (The Gendered Economy)* (Newcastle upon Tyne: Agenda Publishing, 2018).

9 United Nations Office on Drugs and Crime, *Global Report on Trafficking in Persons*, 2012, (Vienna: United Nations Office on Drugs and Crime, 2012).

10 NCVO, 'What Is Commissioning?', 2017. *https://beta.ncvo.org.uk/help-and-guidance/funding-income/delivering-public-services/#commissioning*; Local Partnerships, 'Commissioning in Local Government: A Research Project for Local Partnerships', (London: 2015). PDF available at: *https://localpartnerships.org.uk/wp-content/uploads/2016/05/Commissioning-in-local-government-BD.pdf.*

11 Maddy Coy et al., 'Map of Gaps 2: The postcode lottery of Violence against Women support services in Britain' (London: End Violence Against Women, 2009). *www.researchgate.net/publication/316789565_Map_of_Gaps_2_The_postcode_lottery_of_Violence_Against_Women_support_services_in_Britain*; Lucy Heady et al., 'Understanding the stability and sustainability of the violence against women voluntary sector' (London: Government Equalities Office, 2009). PDF available

at: *https://assets.publishing.service.gov.uk/government/uploads/system/uploads/attachment_data/file/85548/violence-against-women.pdf*

12 Jo Neale and Kathryn Hodges, '"My Head Was Like a Washing Machine on Spin": (Improving) Women's Experiences of Accessing Support', *Dignity: A Journal on Sexual Exploitation and Violence*, Vol 5, No. 3 (December 2020), *doi.org/10.23860/dignity.2020.05.03.03*

13 House of Commons Committee of Public Accounts, 'Financial Sustainability of Local Authorities', (London: House of Commons, 2018). PDF available at: *https://publications.parliament.uk/pa/cm201719/cmselect/cmpubacc/970/970.pdf*; Benjamin Kentish, 'Councils Forced to Use Emergency Cash to Pay for Social Care as Funding Shortfall Grows', *The Independent*, 24 November 2017 *www.independent.co.uk/news/uk/politics/councils-cash-reserves-social-care-funding-crisis-health-budget-a8074911.html*

14 All Party Parliamentary Group on Sexual Violence, 'All-Party Parliamentary Group on Sexual Violence Report into the Funding and Commissioning of Sexual Violence and Abuse Services 2018', (Leeds: Rape Crisis, 2018). PDF available at: *www.basw.co.uk/system/files/resources/report-on-funding-and-commissioning-of-sv-and-abuse-services-2018.pdf*; Reis, 'Life-Changing and Life-Saving: Funding for the women's sector', (Women's Budget Group, 2018). PDF available at: *https://wbg.org.uk/wp-content/uploads/2018/12/WBG-Funding-Report-2.pdf*

15 Neale and Hodges, "My Head Was Like a Washing Machine on Spin", p. 3.

16 Linda Milbourne and Mike Cushman, 'From the third sector to the big society: how changing UK Government policies have eroded third sector trust', *International Journal of Voluntary and Nonprofit Organizations*, Vol 24, No. 2 (2013); Rob Macmillan, *The Third Sector Delivering Public Services* (Birmingham: The Third Research Centre, 2010).

17 Outreach: being available on the streets or locations other than their base on certain days and/or evenings, with staff and volunteers making themselves known to women who may benefit from their support.

18 Hannah Lewis et al., *Faith Responses to Modern Slavery* (Sheffield: The University of Sheffield, 2020). PDF available at: *https://jliflc.com/wp-content/uploads/2020/02/Faith-reponses-to-modern-slavery-2020-Uni-Sheffield-and-Leeds_LowRes.pdf*

19 Norman Blaikie, *Approaches to Social Enquiry: Advancing Knowledge* (Second Edition) (Cambridge: Polity, 2007).

20 Kathryn Hodges, *An Exploration of Decision Making by Women Experiencing Multiple and Complex Needs* (Cambridge: Anglia Ruskin University, 2018); Roger Matthews et al., *Exiting Prostitution: A Study in Female Desistance* (Basingstoke: Palgrave Macmillan, 2014).

21 Hodges, *An Exploration of Decision Making by Women*.

22 Matthews et al., *Exiting Prostitution*.

1
What We Already Know

Intersecting lived experiences: The things that happen to women

It is essential that the quality and access of services for women are improved, particularly for women experiencing multiple and severe disadvantage. For some, the lack of access to services, or the decision to leave them, can cause further harm to their safety and wellbeing.[1] If a helping service is how the community provides support to women and it fails to do so in a way that is helpful, then the implications of this must be understood.

There remains a "high prevalence of institutional misunderstanding" about the needs and experiences of women, particularly in relation to the subtle nature of coercion and abuse they can be subjected to.[2] When women find their local service is not hugely helpful or doesn't make them feel safe (where their only choice is accept or refuse the support on offer), there are then gaps in support and further complexity in navigating systems. There are fatal ramifications for women when they are unable to access effective, trustworthy and reliable support when they need it.[3]

> ### What is 'need' and why is it important?
>
> The term 'need', and its role in enabling access to resources, is interwoven into the fabric of the UK welfare provision and its helping services.
>
> This language of need was embedded in the NHS and Community Care Act 1990, with the initial intention to ensure services responded to and aligned with individual 'need'. Individuals are assessed and defined by their 'need', and this has significant implications for their

access to help and support. **Judgements around who needs a service, or whose 'needs' are too complex for a particular service to handle, have become tied up with resource allocation, cost rationing and control.**[4]

However, 'need' is a difficult concept to define,[5] and **if women's experiences (the things that happen to them) are *not* viewed as needs in law and policy, women will be left without access to help when they require it.** Who gets to define personal need, and what their own (contested) understanding of the term encompasses, has significant implications for potential service users.

For example, in an evaluation of domestic violence and abuse (DVA) provision in the Midlands,[6] service providers remarked on the barriers they had witnessed when trying to support survivors of DVA considered to have complex needs, which included women being portrayed as non-compliant, or 'too-complex' to house or engage with available services.

> *...I can think of one particular woman – all day on the phone trying to find refuge space and we kept getting the same reply that the woman's needs were too high and she would put other women at risk or she would put other children at risk because of her drug taking or mental health issues, and then she was killed. Literally that happened on the Friday [trying to find refuge] and I came back into work on the Monday and she was killed. I can think of six or seven women that we know have been killed at the point of trying to say "I am not safe and I need to go [into refuge]" but their needs were "too high" for those services.*
>
> Support worker[7]

Needs: Complex, multiple, and intersecting?

Sometimes the term 'complex needs' is used to describe those who have had lots of things happen to them for which they would benefit from support. However, it is a term that gives the impression that the individual is responsible for many of the things that have happened to them.

In contrast, **the term 'severe and multiple disadvantage' explains the things that happen to people because of society's actions**.[8] It refocuses attention to the impact society, and all that encompasses, has on individuals.[9]

Adults facing severe and multiple disadvantage are often living at the very margins of society and are less likely to access helping services or benefit from them when they do, finding it difficult to engage with multiple services.[10] It reflects a failure of helping services if individuals have to seek support from a wide range of providers to respond to the multiple things that have happened to them, rather than being able to seek help from a holistic, central provider.[11] This is particularly problematic when we consider how current support provision is siloed according to need.

...she didn't want to know... She was saying to me that she's there to support people that come in for showers and mostly drug addiction, and she doesn't really deal with domestic violence.

Anne[12]

The term 'intersecting experiences' is used in this report, alongside severe and multiple disadvantage, to reflect this awareness and how the things that happen to women are

> interwoven with systems of power, oppression and social inequalities. This reflects the intersectional approach[13] applied in this research, which has provided a useful way to explore the interdependent nature of the things that happen to women.

Understanding the complexity of women's lives and the intersecting nature of the things that happen to them is essential when considering how support can be helpfully provided. This section explores some of the intersecting lived experiences reported by women facing severe and multiple disadvantage. It demonstrates how the things that happen to women interweave and create increasingly complex circumstances. This should be read and understood in the context of the wide range of demographic factors that affect us all, including age, class, ethnicity, culture, education, and so on.

There remains a "high prevalence of institutional misunderstanding" about the needs and experiences of women.

Childhood trauma and mental wellbeing

My mum and biological dad, we lived together for about four years from birth, they used to beat each other up though, and he used to beat me up as well... she accused him of trying to kill me.

Tess[14]

There is now growing understanding about the impact on adults of complex trauma associated with childhood abuse and neglect.[15] Significant numbers of women and men who have been sexually exploited and/or experience multiple and severe disadvantage as an adult have also been victims/survivors of violence and childhood abuse or neglect.[16] Many women involved in prostitution report that this involvement began before they were eighteen years old – in other words, they were a victim of child sexual exploitation, and this exploitation has continued into adulthood.[17]

Childhood abuse and trauma adds to a complex picture of mental wellbeing. Experiencing violence and abuse has a significant long-term impact on mental health and wellbeing.[18]

> *...I am really up and I go down as well, very fast I go up and down, very fast... so you know, much better than I was, because before I was very, very angry, very angry as well, very angry for what happened, I was really angry, and I got more and more angry... and I don't want to be nasty and malicious.*
>
> Judy[19]

We also know that individuals disassociate themselves from their experiences to cope, enabling a kind of protection from the emotional impact of trauma. Dissociation can reduce internal conflict and cognitive dissonance; it is described as "an extreme version of the denial that occurs daily in all sectors of society; bad things are ignored, or we pretend they will go away, or we will call them by another name."[20] However, such dissociation can put individuals at risk of further victimisation in the future as it may cause them to ignore or miss indicators of potential harm.[21]

This process of dissociating from the things that have happened is described to researchers by two women who were involved in, or previously involved in, prostitution.[22]

> *I've got this ability to keep my head completely separated from my body. It's two different entities. Two different bodies and*

one does not interfere with the other. I suspect that the way I was brought up, the childhood, would have facilitated that.

Study participant[23]

But I think I genuinely switch off. I think that they call it disassociation, don't they? And they say that it's a bad thing, but then would it be a good thing if you didn't?

Study participant[24]

Money, debt, and criminal records

Experiences of poverty also make women vulnerable to exploitation and abuse, with many women indicating initial involvement in prostitution being driven by the need to fund accommodation, food and other costs associated with supporting children.[25] In addition, 95% of women who experience domestic abuse report experiencing economic abuse.[26] Debt and financial issues continue to entrap women, preventing them from completing education or training, in turn impacting on their future employment options.[27]

DVA is recognised as playing a major part in female offending,[28] with at least 60% of female offenders who have been supervised in the community or in custody reporting that they have experienced domestic abuse.[29] There are broader associations between victimisation and criminality, with a significant number of women having criminal records resulting from acts of survival, including through involvement in prostitution, illicit drug use, or acquisitive crimes such as theft. Criminal records have a far-reaching impact for women, making it more complicated when trying to create positive change in their lives, particularly when looking for employment.[30]

While numbers of women in prison have steadily increased, this has not been reflected in the nature of the offences committed requiring a custodial sentencing.[31]

Women's involvement in the criminal justice system creates further disadvantage, bringing attention to the cumulative impact of women's intersecting lived experiences.[32] For example, women remanded in prison or on a short sentence risk losing their housing, which is particularly significant for those who are primary carers for young children.[33]

Somewhere safe

It is essential that women can access safe and secure accommodation. Homelessness creates further precarity in the lives of women, increasing isolation and potentially creating harmful dependencies on men.[34] As Judy explains,

> *Come out of jail you've got nowhere to go, you end up here, or you end up back in jail, because you've got nowhere to go... and in the end I got sleeping with somebody or got in somewhere which isn't good for them and putting up with things they shouldn't put up with for a place to stay, sleeping with some old man that's 70 because they've got nowhere to go...*
>
> Judy[35]

> **There is now growing understanding about the impact on adults of complex trauma associated with childhood abuse and neglect.**

A similar situation is echoed by one of the women interviewed by researchers hearing about how women exited prostitution:[36]

> *At the end of the day, he was a customer that I was living with, and even though he wanted me to get clean and that was a condition that I was living there...Another condition was that I was having sex with him regularly. He was an old guy. I didn't particularly want to have sex with him.*
>
> Study participant

When living on the streets, women are further exposed to sexual abuse, violence and stigmatisation. As a result they often conceal themselves from those who exploit, and in doing so are also hidden from helping services.[37] The priority of finding somewhere to sleep each night can overtake concerns about anything else, including attending helping services or programmes of support.

In mixed hostel accommodation, the way women are met and responded to by other residents and staff can leave women feeling unsafe, increasing their vulnerability if they leave and end up sleeping on the streets, on others' sofas, or in crack houses.[38] Here a woman talks about living in a mixed hostel accommodation.[39]

> **95% of women who experience domestic abuse report experiencing economic abuse.**

I'm living in a hostel with all the working girls and junkies, and I hate it. Basically. But there's nothing I can do to change it, except wait to be offered a flat or commit suicide.
Study participant[40]

The precarity in people's lives created by homelessness, nearly always intersecting with other lived experiences, creates opportunities for (further) exploitation. It is reported that most British nationals who become victims of trafficking had been sleeping rough and/or experienced mental illness and/or had a learning disability.[41] If this precarity remains for victims and survivors of modern slavery when they leave the support framework of the National Referral Mechanism[42], the risk of being re-trafficked is particularly high (for example, if someone does not have access to safe and secure accommodation).[43]

Substance use

> *If you see a woman down the street yeah and she might be acting a bit loopy or she might be under the influence of drugs or shouting to herself why don't you stop and think about what that person has been through to make them like that, it could be domestic abuse, could be sexual abuse... they weren't born like that. And they didn't say when they was at school that when I grow up I want to be a drug addict or homeless. Don't be so quick to judge and tarnish people...*
>
> Sally[44]

Drug and alcohol use is reportedly high amongst those involved in prostitution, and DVA survivors are also at a higher risk of substance use.[45] It is impossible to separate cause and effect amongst survivors who use substances and experience mental ill-health.[46] For example, Anne said that she "self-medicated myself from when I was a very young age with heroin"; Sally commented that drinking "helped me cope with being on the streets"; Tina reported that her alcohol use increased steadily after her son was taken into the care of the local authority.[47]

The wider experiences and histories of women must again be appreciated, rather than rushing to neat assumptions that drug use is a particular motivator for involvement in things like prostitution.[48] Frequently, continued use of substances is a way to self-medicate and manage the psychological impact of abuse and exploitation, in addition to finding ways to support a partner's drug and/or alcohol use in complex relationships.[49]

Many helping services state they are unable to support, or only have limited number of places, for those using drugs and/or alcohol, creating further barriers for women already experiencing multiple and severe disadvantage through their intersecting lived experiences. This can leave women unable to access help until they have stopped using substances, with little attention given to the reason why they are using drugs and/or alcohol in the first place.

Being a mother

There needs to be better consideration of women's role as mothers. For women experiencing repeated removal of their children through social services intervention, there is limited aftercare support available.[50]

Rightly embedded within our child protection legislation is the central premise that the child's needs are paramount.[51] However, the needs of women are a lesser consideration – to the point that once involvement of social services with children has ended, so ends the support available for mothers. Women who were experiencing such difficulties that they were unable to care for their child are often left without any support.[52]

> **The precarity in people's lives created by homelessness, nearly always intersecting with other lived experiences, creates opportunities for (further) exploitation.**

My son was taken off me, and my little girl was took into care... I was in such an abusive, abusive domestic violence relationship. I was just such a broken person.

Anne[53]

...Was just used to having my kids around me and all of a sudden I was a single person again and umm...I had a lot to do, because when you go to court you've got so much to do... you're bombarded with appointments... you know.... I really had a lot to do. I was very busy, but very lonely.

Debbie[54]

Children also provide women with the main motivation to seek change in their lives, Anne said that having her child removed by the local authority was like a lightbulb going on, "I was like, this is the wakeup call".[55]

> ...my long-term dream... to get my daughter back and be a good mum, it's not too late, well she's ten now, it's still going to, it's still bad but yeah, I've got to start somewhere...
>
> Jane[56]

Grief, loss, and networks of support

Removal of children is part of a wider experience of grief and loss. In a previous study,[57] women's experiences of grief and loss permeated throughout the interviews. These were experiences that spanned from childhood to present day. Women talked about parents dying when they were children, being abandoned by parents, and their children dying.

> ...when my son died I used to be... I had a temper but I just felt anger against the damn world... I was just thinking why me, what have I done? I must be cursed or something.
>
> Sally[58]

> **Frequently, continued use of substances is a way to self-medicate and manage the psychological impact of abuse and exploitation.**

Rarely are women asked about the grief and loss they have experienced when helping services assess their needs. However, when we think about the attachments and support networks that are lost, the impact on help-seeking is sizeable. Poor care-seeking experiences are often mitigated by support of friends and family.[59]

Very simply, little attention is given to the support that is often needed by many of us to attend appointments, to have someone to walk beside us on difficult journeys. If we pay attention to the experience of grief and loss, and its impact on how women seek help and support, then we better understand that

> **Many helping services state they are unable to support, or only have limited number of places, for those using drugs and/or alcohol.**

many women are left in complex and dangerous circumstances, making difficult choices and decisions without the support from friends and family that many of us benefit from.

Helping services: Understanding why women attend, leave and return

Understanding what is helpful to women when they are seeking help and support is essential. So often we hear that someone 'wasn't motivated enough' to attend a service, or they 'didn't engage' (turn up at the allotted time and speak to an identified keyworker), and frequently they are then 'discharged' from that service. There needs to be greater appreciation of why and how women attend, leave, or return to helping services, and better awareness of the actions practitioners and organisations need to take to create an environment that is deemed safe enough by women so they can benefit from the help available.

> *I was like on the bus here, there, here, there, every day and eventually I was just... Cause mentally I was in a bad way, from my domestic violence and my drinking and my drugs and everything I was just a mess... my head was like a washing machine on spin... you've got to try and concentrate, go to art lesson then go to... this alcohol talk then go to.... and everything*

*is in different parts of the city you know, you've got to go from
there to there to there.*

Jane[60]

Helping services are often organised to respond to a single
need or problem, such as mental wellbeing, substance use or
experiences of domestic abuse. This can lead to fragmented
services – a challenge which is recognised in the repeated
emphasis in policy on multi-agency collaboration and
integrated care.[61]

Services are not only siloed by way of the issues to which
they will respond, but there are variations in access criteria,
intervention, and the time support available. Women with
intersecting lived experiences are expected to attend different
services that respond to the different things that have
happened to them. This can be confusing, impenetrable, and
exhausting.

Knowing you have a need and help is available

Before accessing a service for help and support,
individuals must know the things that have happened to them
are considered 'needs', that they are entitled to support, and
that support is available. Women talk about the things that
happen to them, but (unsurprisingly) rarely refer to their
experiences in the language required by policymakers and
statutory services (i.e. the technical language of need, see
above pp. 32-35).[62]

This requires professionals delivering or developing
services to understand how women understand and explain the
things that have happened to them, and then being clear about
the way support services can help women who have had these
experiences.

Accompanying women to appointments at other helping services is an essential element of effective service delivery. For many women with intersecting lived experiences, being sign-posted to another helping service fails to understand the impact of the things that have happened to them in their previous experience of care-seeking.[63]

> *Megan came with me to my court case, on Monday... she volunteered, you know she said to me can I send a statement, a witness statement about you? And I said are you sure? No, no, I want to, so she did. Then she asked to come... I said you don't have to and she said, then she offered to pay... so, that's someone who cares; she didn't have to do all of that.*
>
> Storm[63]

> *...she's been really supportive like, she met me there, she came with me, saying if that place isn't suitable don't give up... you know we can go on to the computer and look for other centres and things like that.*
>
> Sally[64]

Models of service provision are often based on different assumptions regarding individuals' motivations and behaviour to access help and support. Some projects promote help-seeking while others tend to be more coercive, such as court ordered community rehabilitation programmes, child protection plans, or requirements to follow care plans to access further help and support (such as better housing options).

> **There needs to be greater appreciation of why and how women attend, leave, or return to helping services.**

Many services operate on a conditional basis, such as requiring women to attend appointments at times, frequency, venues, and geographical locations that suit services, yet which are often very hard to fulfil for women whose everyday lives are already challenging and complex. The practical and often coercive demands of service attendance can be very difficult for women.[65]

> *I didn't like going to the Brixton Road project every time because there is too many bad associates for me up there...they all hang out outside just waiting for each other.*
>
> Tess[66]

The geographical location of a service also impacts women's ability to access support, either through transport costs, lack of transport, or because a service is in a place to which a woman does not want to return, either because it brings with it bad memories, or the risk of bumping into people they would rather avoid. Sandy said she chose not to go to a mental health appointment as it was in an area she wanted to avoid because of past experiences.

> *I just didn't turn up... just couldn't do it.*
>
> Sandy[67]

Barriers experienced by DVA survivors seeking help and support

The difficulties and inequalities experienced by DVA survivors when they seek help and support have been recorded across a number of studies.[68] They include not being able to access a service because of its geographical location and economic and social barriers, including those found in language, culture, and disabled accessibility.[69,70] In addition, DVA survivors are also affected by attitudes of

> victim blaming,[71] where they are left feeling culpable for the victimisation they have experienced.

Developing trusting relationships: How women are met and heard

Women, unsurprisingly, 'read' professional carers' behaviour and decide if they are going to help, leaving services, or not returning where they feel the response is negative or unhelpful.[72] For example, Jane said that reading people's body language was one way she was able to overcome her 'trust barrier'.

> *The way... their body language... isn't it, body language I don't know... I can't put it in words... but it's just that feeling... of safety... hope... help... that you're going... that you're looking for...*
> Jane[73]

Women decide if staff and services are trustworthy by noticing body language and assessing whether people seem to care.[74]

> *The way like they used to speak to you like it's just, like the vibe I used to get off her, you know, and when she would speak to me she'd never look me in the eye or just wee things like that.*
> Anne[75]

For women to receive effective support, it is essential that professional caregivers understand the dynamics of help-seeking and respond appropriately.[76] This is particularly important when we consider women's experiences of trauma and previous experiences of help-seeking.

Previous experiences of trauma and unsuccessful attempts at help-seeking is the key context in which women seek support, and in the way they should be met in services.[77] For

Valuing Women

> **Many services operate on a conditional basis, such as requiring women to attend appointments at times, frequency, venues, and geographical locations that suit services.**

many it is a priority to recover from trauma before addressing other concerns in their lives, and relational and trauma-informed care approaches[78] establish principles to improve responses for those seeking help and support.[79]

Those who have experienced violence and abuse in the past due to the "absence of a safe environment" may find the trauma creates obstacles to accessing support,[80] making it essential that places of safety are created for women to promote better outcomes and quality of support. However, a sense of safety is more than just the practical management of a space.

> *It's a safe place for a woman and not only that, you've got people that... people that will go listen to you and do what they say they are going to do.*
>
> Sally[81]

There are several factors that are known to be helpful to women when seeking help and support. Some of these relate to obvious practical issues, such as being able to get to a service, being able to manage services around childcare and avoiding anyone who might make women feel unsafe, and the timings, length, and frequency of appointments. It is also important to women that support staff take time to listen and that they feel they are listened to, and that this is respected and kept confidential.[82]

> *Someone I can unload and tell them how I really feel about what's going on in my life and in confidence and know that it wouldn't be gossiped about...*

Sally[83]

> *I knew that they were there to get me and my kids back together do you know. So then I knew I could be honest and not to be scared and open up and trust them.*

Anne[84]

> *[The service has a] relaxed atmosphere and understanding, it's just the patience, just the patience that the staff have here with you was just, I haven't found it really anywhere else... warm and friendly and I wasn't sure about some of the women in here but I could see how they just felt like they belonged, you could see how they felt like they belonged... It probably made people's behaviour a bit better... than usual... including me as well, it made me a lot calmer when I came here.*

Jasmine[85]

Shaped by faith: Faith-based social care provision

The severe and multiple disadvantage experienced by women is well-documented. However, less is known about the way Christian charities provide support to women, which this study seeks to explore. FBOs[86] are shaped by faith or underpinned by faith tradition, although the work they do is not necessarily overtly religious.[87] As previous Theos research has shown, FBOs are not homogenous groups – in terms of either their motivation or approaches – and generalisations cannot be made about their activities or impact.[88] However, they are frequently supporting individuals who could be considered the most marginalised in our society.

It is often suggested that FBOs are filling gaps left by the withdrawal of welfare state provision from public life, and this role has also been widely unpacked in previous Theos research, as well as a range of academic studies.[89]

In many cases, this 'gap filling' is the most valuable contribution FBOs can make, and indeed, many FBOs appear to offer services very similar to the secular counterparts they are replacing or supplementing. The authors of a previous study exploring the role of faith in social care services observed that:

> *Faith matters in important ways, especially in terms of resources and the approach to programs and clients... we find that faith is not a good predictor of how an agency operates and its interactions with clients... only a relatively small percentage of all FBOs are distinctively different from secular agencies or other types of FBOs.*[90]

These comments are also reflected in studies which have sought to understand the ways that faith shapes service delivery and is experienced by service users.[91] Interviewees who accessed services for homeless people reported "no obvious difference in quality or integrity of care provided by staff in projects that were known to be faith-based or secular."[92]

> **Theos research has shown that FBOs are not homogenous groups – in terms of either their motivation or approaches – and generalisations cannot be made about their activities or impact.**

It is suggested that this is partly because FBOs must carefully manage the implications for accessing government funding alongside the values of their organisation and way the service operates. This is also the case for secular organisations operating in complex political spaces, such as those supporting refugees. The reality is that "many voluntary agencies now compete in civil markets where smart just-in-time projects are in much more demand than complex interventions with unknown or not measurable outcomes."[93] To clarify, both secular and FBO third-sector organisations compete in civil markets and are delivering these smart just-in time projects. It is useful here to echo comments made in another study, that "it is important to highlight that we and our participants do not view the world as one made up of two dichotomous groups of service providers – some faith-based, some secular."[94]

At the same time, various studies have suggested that FBOs are more likely to favour unconditional approaches to providing support, aligning with their ideals of unconditional hospitality and care, as opposed to highly interventionist approaches that tend to be endorsed by Government.[95]

These unconditional approaches, or non-interventionist provision, tend to have an open-door policy, whereas interventionist services require individuals to engage with programmes of support. Whilst some may critique the unconditional approaches for seeming to leave individuals to continue with behaviours that are harming their wellbeing, it is understood that those experiencing multiple and severe disadvantage are more likely to access unconditional rather than interventionist provision.[96]

> **Many FBOs appear to offer services very similar to the secular counterparts they are replacing or supplementing.**

Women's experiences of help-seeking from Christian charities

There is little previous research focusing on how FBOs support women experiencing multiple and severe disadvantage. However, as noted above, FBOs' preference to provide unconditional support is helpful to women, particularly for those who have extensive histories of trauma.

The research here explores how Christian charities provide help and support to women with intersecting lived experiences and what can be learned from this. Part Two sets out the four themes that emerged from the in-depth original research conducted in 2020-21, where the report authors heard from 21 staff and volunteers based at six charities.

> At the same time, various studies have suggested that FBOs are more likely to favour unconditional approaches to providing support.

1 Kathryn Hodges and Sarah Burch, 'Multiple and Intersecting Experiences of Women in Prostitution: Improving Access to Helping Services' Dignity Vol 4, No. 2 (2019); Lyndsey Harris and Kathryn Hodges, 'Responding to Complexity: improving service provision for survivors of domestic abuse with 'complex needs' *Journal of Gender Based Violence*, Vol 3, No. 2, pp. 167-184; Matthews et al., *Exiting Prostitution...* (op. cit. Introduction p.14)

2 Jean Corston, *The Corston Report* (London: Home Office, 2007), *webarchive. nationalarchives.gov.uk/ukgwa/20130128112038/ http://www.justice.gov.uk/ publications/docs/corston-report-march-2007.pdf*

3 Neale and Hodges, '"My Head Was Like a Washing Machine on Spin..."; Harris and Hodges, 'Responding to Complexity...'; Hodges and Burch, 'Multiple and Intersecting Experiences of Women in Prostitution...'; Matthews, 'Policing Prostitution: Ten Years On', *The British Journal of Criminology* Vol 45, No. 6 (2005), pp. 877-895.

4 Mary Godfrey and Gill Callaghan, *Exploring Unmet Need: The Challenge of a User-Centred Response* (York: York Publishing Services for the Joseph Rowntree Foundation, 2000).

5 Graham Smith, *Social Need* (London: Routledge and Kegan Paul, 1980); Jonathan Bradshaw, 'A Taxonomy of Social Need', in *Jonathan Bradshaw on Social Policy: Selected Writings 1972-2011* (York: University of York, 1972).

6 Dr Lyndsey Harris, *Response to Complexity (R2C): Final Evaluation* (Nottingham: The University of Nottingham, 2016); Harris and Hodges, 'Responding to Complexity...'

9 Harris and Hodges, 'Responding to Complexity...'

10 Harris, Response to Complexity (R2C): Final Evaluation; Glen Bramley and Suzanne Fitzpatrick et al., Hard Edges: Mapping Severe and Multiple Disadvantage (London: Lankelly Chase Foundation, 2015), *lankellychase.org.uk/ wp-content/uploads/2015/07/Hard-Edges-Mapping-SMD-2015.pdf*

11 Harris and Hodges, 'Responding to Complexity...'

12 Cabinet Office, *Reaching Out: An Action Plan on Social Exclusion* (London: Her Majesty's Stationary Office, 2006).

13 Ann Rosenberg et al., *A Literature Review on Multiple and Complex Needs*, (Edinburgh: Scottish Executive Social Research, 2007), *www.researchgate.net/ publication/242483070_A_Literature_Review_on_Multiple_and_Complex_Needs*; Jennifer Rankin and Sue Regan, *Meeting Complex Needs: The Future of Social Care* (London: IPPR & Turning Point, 2004); J. Keene, Clients with Complex Needs: *Interprofessional Practice* (Oxford: Blackwell Science Ltd, 2001), *doi. org/10.1002/9780470690352*

14 The concept of intersectionality is useful as a way of exploring women's lives: it broadly refers to the interaction between multiple forms of oppression.

15 Hodges, *An Exploration of Decision Making...*

16 Hodges, *An Exploration of Decision Making...*

17 Bramley et al., *Hard Edges...* (op. cit. Part One) .

18 Coy, 'Introduction: Prostitution, Harm and Gender Inequality...'; Matthews et al., *Exiting Prostitution...* (op. cit. Introduction p.14); Suzanne Fitzpatrick, Glen Bramley, and Sarah Johnsen, 'Pathways into Multiple Exclusion Homelessness in Seven UK Cities', *Urban Studies* Vol 50, No. 1 (2013), pp. 148–168, *doi.org/10.1177/0042098012452329*; Theresa McDonagh, *Tackling homelessness and exclusions:Understanding complex lives* (York: Joseph Rowntree Foundation, 2011); Maddy Coy, 'Young Women, Local Authority Care and Selling Sex: Findings from Research', *The British Journal of Social Work* Vol 38, No. 7 (2008), p. 1408–24, *doi.org/10.1093/bjsw/bcm049*; M. Hester and N. Westmarland, 'Tackling Street Prostitution : Towards a Holistic Approach' (London: Home Office, 2004), *dro.dur.ac.uk/2557/*

19 Coy, 'Joining the Dots...'; Matthews et al., *Exiting Prostitution...* (op. cit. Introduction p.14)

20 Sara Scott et al., 'Violence, abuse and mental health in England (REVA project, Briefing 1)', 2015, *www.natcen.ac.uk/revabriefing1*

21 Hodges, *An Exploration of Decision Making...*

22 Colin A. Ross, Melissa Farley and Harvey L. Schwartz, 'Dissociation among Women in Prostitution', in Prostitution, *Trafficking and Traumatic Stress*, ed. Melissa Farley (Abingdon: Routledge, 2004), p. 206.

23 Ross, Farley and Schwartz, *'Dissociation among Women in Prostitution'...*

24 Matthews et al., *Exiting Prostitution...* (op. cit. Introduction p.14)

25 Matthews et al., *Exiting Prostitution...* (op. cit. Introduction p.14) p. 33–34.

26 Matthews et al., *Exiting Prostitution...* (op. cit. Introduction p.14)p. 34.

27 Matthews et al., *Exiting Prostitution...* (op. cit. Introduction p.14); Hester and Westmarland, 'Tackling Street Prostitution...'; Rochelle L. Dalla, 'Night Moves: A Qualitative Investigation of Street-Level Sex Work', Psychology of Women Quarterly Vol 26, No. 1 (March 2002), p. 63–73, *doi.org/10.1111/1471-6402.00044*

28 Surviving Economic Abuse, 'Statistics on Financial and Economic Abuse', 2020, *survivingeconomicabuse.org/wp-content/uploads/2020/11/Statistics-on-economic-abuse.pdf*

29 Matthews et al., *Exiting Prostitution...* (op. cit. Introduction p.14); Hester and Westmarland, 'Tackling Street Prostitution...'

30 Judith Rumgay et al, 'When Victims Become Offenders: In Search of Coherence in Policy and Practice', *Family & Intimate Partner Violence* Quarterly Vol 3, No. 1 (2010), p. 47–64.

31 Ministry of Justice, 'Female Offender Strategy' (Ministry of Justice, 2018), *assets.publishing.service.gov.uk/government/uploads/system/uploads/attachment_data/file/719819/female-offender-strategy.pdf*

32 Heather Harvey, Laura Brown, and Lisa Young, *'I'm No Criminal': Examining the impact of prostitution-specific criminal records on women seeking to exit prostitution*, (London: nia, 2017).

33 Prison Reform Trust and Women in Prison, 'Home truths: housing for women in the criminal justice system' (Prison Reform Trust, 2016, rev. 2018), *www.prisonreformtrust.org.uk/portals/0/documents/home%20truths%20june%202018.pdf*; Anne Worrall and Loraine Gelsthorpe, '"What works" with women offenders: The past 30 years', Probation Journal Vol 56, No. 4 (December 2009), p. 329–45, *doi.org/10.1177/0264550509346538*; Fawcett Society, Women and the criminal justice system (London: Fawcett Society, 2004).

34 Bramley et al., *Hard Edges…* (op. cit. Part One)

35 Prison Reform Trust and Women in Prison, 'Home truths: housing for women…'

36 Prison Reform Trust and Women in Prison, 'Home truths: housing for women…'; Corston, *The Corston Report…*

37 Hodges, *An Exploration of Decision Making…*

38 Matthews et al., *Exiting Prostitution…* p. 51, (op. cit. Introduction p.14).

39 Joanne Bretherton and Nicholas Pleace, *Women and Rough Sleeping: A Critical Review of Current Research and Methodology* (York: University of York, 2018

40 Hodges, *An Exploration of Decision Making…*; Matthews et al., Exiting Prostitution… (op. cit. Introduction p.14)

41 Matthews et al., *Exiting Prostitution…* (op. cit. Introduction p.14)

42 The National Referral Mechanism is the UK government's interpretation of its duty under the EU Anti-trafficking Directive 2011/36/EU to "establish appropriate mechanisms aimed at early identification of, assistance to and support for victims, in cooperation with relevant support organisations." In the UK the NRM is a framework to identify victims. Matthews et al., Exiting Prostitution… (op. cit. Introduction p.14) p. 51.

43 Miranda Keast, 'Understanding and Responding to Modern Slavery within the Homelessness Sector' (London: Homeless Link, 2017), *www.antislaverycommissioner.co.uk/media/1115/understanding-and-responding-to-modern-slavery-within-the-homelessness-sector.pdf*; Homeless Link, 'Trafficking and Forced Labour: Guidance for Frontline Homelessness Services' (London: Homeless Link, 2016).

44 Miranda Keast, *Understanding and Responding to Modern Slavery…*'; Homeless Link, 'Trafficking and Forced Labour… see above comment

45 Hodges, *An Exploration of Decision Making...*

46 Matthews et al., *Exiting Prostitution...* (op. cit. Introduction p.14); Laura Brown and Ruth Breslin, *Cycles of harm: Problematic alcohol use amongst women involved in prostitution* (London: Alcohol Research UK, 2013), *alcoholchange.org.uk/publication/cycles-of-harm-problematic-alcohol-use-amongst-women-involved-in-prostitution*; Against Violence and Abuse, Complicated Matters: a toolkit addressing domestic and sexual violence, substance use and mental ill-health (London: AVA, 2013), *avaproject.org.uk/wp/wp-content/uploads/2013/05/AVA-Toolkit-2018reprint.pdf*; Hester and Westmarland, 'Tackling Street Prostitution...'

47 Kylee Trevillion et al., 'Experiences of Domestic Violence and Mental Disorders: A Systematic Review and Meta-Analysis', *PLoS ONE Vol 7*, No. 12 (December 2012), p. 1–12.

48 Hodges, *An Exploration of Decision Making...*

49 Brown and Breslin, *Cycles of Harm...*

50 Julie Bindel et al., *Breaking down the barriers: A study of how women exit prostitution* (London: Eaves, 2012); Amy M. Young, Carol Boyd, and Amy Hubbell, 'Prostitution, Drug Use, and Coping with Psychological Distress', *Journal of Drug Issues* Vol 30, No. 4 (October 2000), p. 789–800, *doi/10.1177/002204260003000407*

51 Katie McCracken et al., *Evaluation of Pause: Research Report* (London: Department for Education, July 2017), *www.gov.uk/government/uploads/system/uploads/attachment_data/file/625374/Evaluation_of_Pause.pdf*; Karen Broadhurst et al., 'Connecting Events in Time to Identify a Hidden Population: Birth Mothers and Their Children in Recurrent Care Proceedings in England', *British Journal of Social Work* Vol 45, No. 8 (December 2015) p. 2241–60, *doi.org/10.1093/bjsw/bcv130*

52 'Children Act 1989', *www.legislation.gov.uk/ukpga/1989/41/contents*

53 Broadhurst et al., 'Connecting Events in Time...'

54 Hodges, *An Exploration of Decision Making...*

55 Hodges, *An Exploration of Decision Making...*

56 Hodges, *An Exploration of Decision Making...*

57 Hodges, *An Exploration of Decision Making...*

58 Hodges, *An Exploration of Decision Making...*

59 Hodges, *An Exploration of Decision Making...*

60 Una McCluskey, To Be Met as a Person: *The Dynamics of Attachment in Professional Encounters* (London: Karnac, 2005).

61 Hodges, 'An Exploration of Decision Making by Women...'

62 The King's Fund, 'How Far Has the Government Gone towards Integrating Care?', 2015), *www.kingsfund.org.uk/projects/verdict/how-far-has-government-gone-towards-integrating-care*

63 Hodges and Burch, 'Multiple and Intersecting Experiences of Women in Prostitution...

64 Hodges, *An Exploration of Decision Making...*

65 Hodges, *An Exploration of Decision Making...*

66 Hodges, *An Exploration of Decision Making...*

67 K Rummery, 'Partnership Working and Tackling Violence Against Women. Violence Against Women: Current Theory and Practice' in Nancy Lombard (ed) *Violence Against Women: Current Theory and Practice in Domestic Abuse, Sexual Violence and Exploitation* (London: Jessica Kingsley, 2013), p. 213.

68 Hodges, *An Exploration of Decision Making...*

69 Hodges, *An Exploration of Decision Making...*

70 Harris and Hodges, 'Responding to Complexity...'; Emma Howarth and Amanda Robinson, 'Responding Effectively to Women Experiencing Severe Abuse: Identifying Key Components of a British Advocacy Intervention', *Violence Against Women* Vol 22 No. 1 (2016, *doi.org/10.1177/1077801215597789*)

71 Surviving Economic Abuse, *Statistics on Financial and Economic Abuse*; Melanie McCarry et al., 'The Potential for Co-Production in Developing Violence against Women Services in Wales', *Social Policy and Society* Vol 17, No. 2 (April 2018), p. 193–208, *doi.org/10.1017/S1474746417000070*; Julie McGarry, Chris Simpson, and Kathryn Hinchliff-Smith, 'The impact of domestic abuse for older women: a review of the literature', *Health & Social Care in the Community* Vol 19, No. 1 (January 2011), p. 3–14, *doi.org/10.1111/j.1365-2524.2010.00964.x*

72 Ravi K. Thiara, Gill Hague, and Audrey Mullender, 'Losing out on both counts: disabled women and domestic violence', *Disability & Society* Vol 26, No. 6 (October 2011), p. 757–71, *doi.org/10.1080/09687599.2011.602867*; Jill Radford, Lynne Harne, and Joy Trotter, 'Disabled women and domestic violence as violent crime', *Practice* Vol 18, No. 4 (2006), p. 233–46, *doi.org/10.1080/09503150601025204*

73 Sandra Walklate, *Gender, Crime and Criminal Justice* (London: Routledge, 2013).

74 Trauma-informed methods of working are "based upon an understanding of the harmful effects of traumatic experiences together with fundamental principles of compassion and respect." (Rachel Witkin & Katy Robjant, *The Trauma-informed Code of Conduct* (London: Helen Bamber Foundation, 2018) p1). Hodges and Burch, 'Multiple and Intersecting Experiences of Women in Prostitution...'

75 Hodges, *An Exploration of Decision Making...*

76 Hodges and Burch, 'Multiple and Intersecting Experiences of Women in Prostitution...'

77 Hodges, *An Exploration of Decision Making...*

78 McCluskey, *To Be Met as a Person...*

79 Denise E. Elliott et al., 'Trauma-informed or trauma-denied: Principles and implementation of trauma-informed services for women', *Journal of Community Psychology* Vol 33, No. 4 (July 2005), p. 461–477, *doi.org/10.1002/jcop.20063*; Elizabeth K. Hopper, Ellen L. Bassuk, and Jeffrey Olivet, 'Shelter from the Storm: Trauma-Informed Care in Homelessness Services Settings', *The Open Health Services and Policy Journal* Vol 3 (2010), p. 80–100.

80 Angela Sweeney et al., 'A paradigm shift: relationships in trauma-informed mental health services', *BJPsych Advances* Vol 24, No. 5 (September 2018), p. 319–333, *doi.org/10.1192/bja.2018.29*; Angela Sweeney et al., 'Trauma-informed mental healthcare in the UK: what is it and how can we further its development?', Mental Health Review Journal Vol 21, No. 3 (September 2016), p. 174–192, *doi.org/10.1108/MHRJ-01-2015-0006*; Judith Lewis Herman, Trauma and Recovery, (New York: BasicBooks, 2015).

81 Elliott et al., 'Trauma-Informed or Trauma-Denied...'

82 This study focuses on Christian charities specifically, but they are mostly considered in the literature more broadly as faith-based organisations.

83 Hodges, *An Exploration of Decision Making...*

84 Hodges, *An Exploration of Decision Making...*

85 Hodges, *An Exploration of Decision Making...*

86 Hodges, *An Exploration of Decision Making...*

87 Hodges, *An Exploration of Decision Making...*

88 Margaret Harris, Peter Halfpenny, and Colin Rochester, 'A Social Policy Role for Faith-Based Organisations? Lessons from the UK Jewish Voluntary Sector', *Journal of Social Policy* Vol 32, No. 1 (January 2003), p. 93–112, *doi.org/10.1017/S0047279402006906*; Paul Bickley, *The Problem of Proselytism* (London: Theos, 2015), *www.theosthinktank.co.uk/cmsfiles/archive/files/Problem%20of%20Proselytism%20web%20version.pdf*

89 Justin Beaumont and Paul Cloke, 'Introduction to the Study of Faith-Based Organisations and Exclusion in European Cities', in Beaumont, Justin and Paul Cloke (ed), *Faith-Based Organisations and Exclusion in European Cities*, (Bristol: The Policy Press, 2012).

90 Hannah Rich, *Growing Good; Growth, Social Action and Discipleship in the Church of England* (London: Theos, 2020); Madeleine Pennington, The Church and Social Cohesion: Connecting Communities and Serving People (London: Theos, 2020); Nick Spencer, *Doing Good: A Future for Christianity in the 21st Century* (London:

Theos, 2016); Bickley, Paul, *Good Neighbours: How Churches Help Communities Flourish* (London: Theos, 2014), *www.theosthinktank.co.uk/cmsfiles/Reportfiles/ Good-Neighbours-Report-CUF-Theos-2014.pdf*. José Luis Romanillos, Justin Beaumont, and Mustafa Sen, 'State-Religion Relations and Welfare Regimes in Europe', in Beaumont, Justin and Paul Cloke (ed), *Faith-Based Organisations and Exclusion in European Cities*, (Bristol: The Policy Press, 2012).

91 Steven Rathgeb Smith, John P. Bartkowski, and Susan Grettenberger, *A Comparative View of the Role and Effect of Faith in Social Services*, (Albany: Rockefeller Institute of Government, State University of New York, 2006), p. 24–26.

92 Sarah Johnsen, 'Where's the "Faith" in "Faith-Based" Organisations? The Evolution and Practice of Faith-Based Homelessness Services in the UK', *Journal of Social Policy* Vol 43, No. 2 (April 2014), p. 413–30, *doi.org/10.1017/ S0047279413001001*; Kristin M. Ferguson et al., 'Perceptions of Faith and Outcomes in Faith-Based Programs for Homeless Youth: A Grounded Theory Approach', *Journal of Social Service Research* Vol 33, no. 4 (2007), p. 25–43, *doi.org/10.1300/J079v33n04_03*; Steven Rathgeb Smith, John P. Bartkowski, and Susan Grettenberger, 'A Comparative View of the Role and Effect of Faith...'; Malcolm L Goggin and Deborah A. Orth, *How Faith-Based and Secular Organizations Tackle Housing for the Homeless* (Albany: Rockerfeller Institute of Government, State University of New York, 2002).

93 Johnsen, 'Where's the "Faith" in "Faith-Based" Organisations?...', p. 424.

94 Ingo Bode, 'Disorganized welfare mixes: voluntary agencies and new governance regimes in Western Europe', *Journal of European Social Policy* Vol 16, No. 4 (November 2006), p. 354, *doi.org/10.1177/0958928706068273*

95 Lewis et al., 'Faith Responses to Modern Slavery', p. 14 (op. cit. Introduction).

96 Paul Cloke, Sarah Johnsen, and Jon May, 'Exploring Ethos? Discourses of "Charity" in the Provision of Emergency Services for Homeless People', *Environment and Planning A: Economy and Space* Vol 37, No. 3 (March 2005), p. 385–402, *doi.org/10.1068/a36189*; Johnsen, 'Where's the "Faith" in "Faith-Based" Organisations?...'; Rich, *Growing Good...*; Pennington, *The Church and Social Cohesion...*; Bickley, Good Neighbours...; Johnsen, 'Where's the "Faith" in "Faith-Based" Organisations?...'

97 Johnsen, 'Where's the "Faith" in "Faith-Based" Organisations?...'

2
Finding Out More

How, then, do Christian services meet women experiencing multiple and severe disadvantage, and what can be learned from their practices? We carried out 21 in-depth interviews with staff and volunteers at six Christian charities supporting women experiencing severe and multiple disadvantage; these interviews were analysed thematically, and the research brought light to the elements of care that were distinctive, if not unique, to FBOs.

This in-depth study is a snapshot of the way staff and volunteers talk about their experiences of providing support to women at a Christian charity, it is not comparing FBO and secular care provision, and the findings should be read in this context.

The four themes identified explore: how services understand the lived experiences of women and the priority of creating environments and interactions of trust and safety; the way they value women; the role of prayer in their work; and the tensions and opportunities involved in resourcing support.

To trust and be trusted

And I think the women that we get, who are survivors... they've devised lots of strategies to deal with abnormal behaviour.

Katy

The most difficult thing for me in this job is when people find it difficult to accept that their life can change. Because of the abuse that they went through, they find it difficult to believe that people are helping them out and are there to help them genuinely.

Angela

That trust is so essential, when there's not trust, like things will happen, you know, [when] there's no trust, you can set all the goals, you can make a plan, you can do all those things. But if that trust isn't there, the things aren't going to happen.

Margaret

For help and support to be beneficial to women, they have to feel that they can trust the people providing help and support.[1] The things that happen to women adversely affect how they trust others to help them, including those in helping organisations. It is essential for staff and volunteers to understand how this trust is eroded through the things that happen to women, including previous poor experiences of help and support. The staff and volunteers involved in this study explain some of the things they needed to consider and do to be trusted by the women they were there to support.

> **Housing, without doubt, remains a key priority for women and an area of support that was consistently found wanting in this study.**

As illustrated earlier in this report, it is not enough to just provide a helping service. There needs to be detailed understanding of women's intersecting lived experiences and how safe and secure environments and interactions can be developed. Developing trusting relationships, as Angela, Katy and Margaret explain above, is essential to help engender positive change in women's lives.

The things that happen

Whilst we were unable to hear from women directly, we did hear from staff and volunteers about the things that happened to the women they supported. These accounts reflect much of what is repeatedly recorded, and outlined earlier in this report, about women's experiences of multiple and severe disadvantage.

Lydia and Alice commented on the multiplicity of things that happen to women, and how a failure of support services to respond effectively prevents women from having access to the help and support that they need. Housing, without doubt, remains a key priority for women and an area of support that was consistently found wanting in this study.

> *Lots of issues around housing obviously, maybe it's not obvious, I don't know...drug addictions, and then domestic abuse.*
>
> Lydia

> *...mental health is just a massive... Especially with the women we work with...so you know we refer women into mental health (services) and when they hear about the drugs, they'll go - get yourself sorted, but that's not really possible... So we keep hearing dual diagnosis (services), but we're not actually seeing it really...(it's) a big thing, because, because of all the trauma and everything.*
>
> Alice

Staff and volunteers consistently report the exploitation, violence and abuse experienced by the women they supported.

> *I think it was either a punter or her boyfriend or something and basically in her words you know, he'd given her a good slapping and I think she had like a broken rib...but she was so just like you know, just like dismissive of it when I mentioned it...it's kind of like that's what I deserve...*
>
> Sarah

> *It never ceases to amaze me how the scales fall off women's eyes quite quickly...they go from thinking everything's their fault*

to thinking, actually, maybe I'm not so rubbish, after all... I find it quite scary how some really obvious things aren't obvious to someone that's been in that kind of situation for years and years.
Katy

Again, these experiences are intertwined with prior bad experiences of support services. Eva sets out how these previous negative experiences of seeking help lead to further despair. This in turn has significant implications when seeking help in the future, and whether women can trust and have confidence in those who are purportedly there to help.[2]

...evidencing domestic abuse is really difficult. Particularly if the woman's absolutely petrified of a perpetrator, and is afraid to report it, hasn't been heard in the past, hasn't had good experiences of social services or, or other agencies. And so, you know, reluctant to work with them... So they despair, they despair of the courts, they despair of the police, not turning up, of not, of not supporting, legal costs...getting Legal Aid, fighting in court, or getting the housing they need to be safe. It goes on. There's quite a lot of barriers, and it's still very difficult for the victims.
Eva

> **Staff and volunteers again talk about the well-documented need for responsive holistic services for women.**

Isolation

Diversity of language, literacy levels, immigration status, cultural variance and disability amongst women can lead to isolation and challenges when seeking support, if services and staff are unable to respond. Such isolation is in itself something that can be abused and exploited. It is hard to seek help if you don't know it is there or can't speak the language to communicate the danger you are in. There are further methods used by those who exploit women to isolate them, including removing passports, limiting access to friends and family, financial exploitation and withholding wages, creating fear about the police and other authority figures, and threats of deportation and harm to family.

Kate talks about how her team try to navigate language barriers through information cards they include in gift bags to Thai women in massage parlours.

> *We hope and pray that they do read the information in there, we try and make it as clear and as straightforward as possible in either Thai or Chinese... hopefully ladies can actually read them. Because...we don't know literacy levels, but we have to do something...*
>
> Kate

Sara talks about the bank of volunteer translators they rely on to provide support to women:

> *They come from very different countries, sometimes it's even like communicating the basic stuff. It's very, very difficult because of language barriers.*
>
> Sara

Eva goes on to explain how "financial difficulties, transport, childcare needs, that sort of thing" also impact women's ability to access the help and support on offer at their centres. This again is a consistently reported challenge for women when needing to access support services. They frequently have to travel to multiple services at times that are difficult to manage because of other responsibilities such as childcare.

Staff and volunteers again talk about the well-documented need for responsive holistic services for women, where helping services are preferably based together, are accessible, have childcare, and flexible hours and approaches to service delivery. There are various examples of wraparound care and women's services hubs being piloted under various initiatives,[3] but "women's advocacy services must be restored, underpinned by a secure and sustainable specialist women's sector, and more closely integrated into the package of care provided by statutory agencies."[4] For some, services coming to where the women are is far more helpful.

> *The biggest challenges for the on-street women is just the total chaos that they live in... just simple things like booking appointments, or agreeing to meet...you can agree to meet somebody for coffee... and 9 times out of 10, you know, they won't turn up and you just have to keep pitching up...and hope that on the 10th time, they will turn up.*
>
> Sarah

Too complex

Lydia comments that women they help are frequently considered 'too complex' to access support. She notes that women have to stop using substances before they can access better accommodation or mental health services, which they would benefit from to help address the trauma they have experienced. This is particularly difficult when substance use can be self-medication as a coping mechanism[5].

> **Women are frequently considered 'too complex' to access support.**

When women have more than one thing happening to them which doesn't fit with the single-issue approach of the majority of helping services, then they are left without holistic support to recover. Accounts of women being considered 'too complex' for support, and then facing further exploitation because of this precarity has been documented elsewhere, as mentioned earlier in this report (pp. 32-35, 39-41). The following comment from Alice outlines the reality of this situation,

> *So we will often refer, let's just say to housing for example, and they'll come back and say, oh their needs are too complex. So who is going to help? None of the hostels' accommodation in (this city) are geared up for women, it's mainly male, but with women in there...and our research proved that's where a lot of survival sex starts.*
>
> Alice

There have been several attempts to challenge and address the view that some women (and men) are too complex to support.[6] Much of the complexity sits with the way helping services are offered, and there has been some success found in projects that help women to navigate the different provision they are expected to access.[7]

Invisible

As explored earlier in this report, the things that happen to women are multiple and intersecting; they are not single issues or concerns that can be responded to neatly. Jackie comments that the biggest challenge in providing help and support to women was how to help women "break the cycle...homelessness, drugs, prostitution, maybe shoplifting".

> **The things that happen to women are multiple and intersecting; they are not single issues or concerns that can be responded to neatly.**

Whilst sometimes women are seen as too complex to receive the support available, there are other times where their needs are rendered invisible by the way policies and practices ignore the lived experience of women experiencing multiple and severe disadvantage.

Women are "present in the homeless population, in much greater numbers than is generally assumed."[8] Alice and Lydia outlined how women are limited in their access to housing support through the categorisation of rough sleeping in local policy and guidance. It is another area where policy responds to the male majority, and women are hidden from sight. Women are further isolated and left with difficult choices in managing their own safety, putting them at risk of further exploitation and abuse.[9]

> *A lot of our women that we support sofa surf, as opposed to sleep rough...They don't get classed as the most vulnerable because they're not rough sleeping, but.... but to us sofa surfing and the cost of sofa surfing is horrendous.*
>
> Alice

Alice goes on to explain,

> *We have one delightful quote from a lady saying about waking up to something stuck in one end or the other.... that kind of thing... It's just presumed you can be used in that way to get a bed...they are not treated as a priority, but most of the women won't go in the hostels and I don't blame them...*
>
> Alice

The safety, or otherwise, of women in hostels is well reported, but underlying this there seems to be an acceptance of women being further exploited when they seek help and support.

> *In one of the hostels we've had... I think it's five women have been raped in the hostel in the past year. How is a place getting funded when that's happening? It's... and they're the women we know [about].*
>
> Lydia

For women who have already experienced trauma and exploitation, an environment where they are exposed to further risk of harm is at odds with what is needed for their recovery. This is a failure to respect them as a human being who needs safe shelter.

The most difficult thing: to trust and be trusted

Sarah and Sara set out the way women have experienced relationships, and the impact this has on their ability to trust others. It takes time to build this trust in order to enable an effective working relationship and provide the support women need to recover from trauma. As Sara underlines, time to recover from trauma is very limited in the current systems of help and support. Yet for many women this is essential before they can try to address other concerns.

> *And then the women on the street in particular, most of their relationships are just really messed up...they're based on use, you know, either men using them or you know them using like other people.*
>
> Sarah

> *At the beginning, it's difficult to build a relationship of trust... Because they had terrible*

> **Participants talk about funding which gives them greater freedoms in the way they provide support to women; enabling them to work in a way that doesn't respond to particular outcomes or key performance indicators linked to short term funding.**

> *experience. Sometimes they never had, I guess, a positive memory of [a] nice and positive relationship. So sometimes it is difficult to start...building a relationship of trust with them...recovering from those traumatic experiences...the system in general, doesn't allow them to take the time that they ideally need to...fully recover from that experience.*
>
> Sara

This reflection below by Lydia, talks about how the little things make a difference, that something that is just a basic act of human goodwill and kindness can have such an impact on others.

> *One of the things that I found strangely, very painful, is... when the women on the street have told me something I've done for them, that in the grand scheme of things is nothing...a woman who said to me - you let me go sleep in your car outside the chemist while we were waiting for the chemist to come back to get on her first dose of methadone. - and I'm like, yeah, that's nothing, that is nothing. And you're telling people that I did this, like it's some great thing.*
>
> Lydia

> ❝
>
> **Amongst wider discussions about beliefs and values, staff and volunteers frequently describe how they meet women as meeting women in the image of God.**

We know from previous research that the little things matter, that women look to test how trustworthy and reliable support workers are, for example through the way that they are met and if staff and volunteers do the things that they have promised to do.[10]

In this study staff and volunteers frequently talk about the flexibility they have in their work. For example, staff can be flexible with their time. They can keep showing up week after week with what elsewhere might be considered limited success. They also talk about funding which gives them greater freedoms in the way they provide support to women; enabling them to work in a way that doesn't respond to particular outcomes or key performance indicators linked to short term funding. They can meet and support women where they are and in a way that is helpful to them.

This broadly reflects the literature in terms of the things that have happened to women, and in relation to what we know about how women experiencing multiple and severe disadvantage seek help and support. Trust and consistency are essential.

Staff and volunteers talk about what they do to create environments of trust and safety for women, and where they feel that they are lacking. Understanding the things that happen to women and how these things impact on their help-seeking is the first step to creating environments that feel secure. The next section explores how these environments are formed, through the way women are valued.

Valuing women

Amongst wider discussions about beliefs and values, staff and volunteers frequently describe how they meet women as meeting women in the image of God. Interviewees make frequent reference to how the idea of "going the extra mile", taken from the Bible (Matthew 5.41), informs their work. Women are to be cherished as individuals who are equals, and staff and volunteers talk about the need to be consistently committed in their support for women.

> **The values that really stick out to me...one of the biggest ones I think is valuing the individual and valuing people in their God-given image, you know, [valuing] people's like, they're uniquely made in the image of God, and because of that, they have insurmountable worth.**

When asked, most staff and volunteers find it difficult to verbalise the values of the organisations they work for or explain how they inform their work. Participants say it is hard to put the values into words, or easily bring them to mind. However, what they do talk about is how they bring their own beliefs and values to the role.

Those who don't identify as having a Christian faith explain how their personal values are represented in the work they do. Additionally, one volunteer explains that she sees the values of the Christian charity she works for as replicating the competency standards of the community studies qualification she is completing. Another staff member talks about how the Christian values of the organisation translate to her Muslim faith.

Jo reflects on her own values of caring for others and how this informs her ideas of setting up a safehouse for women who have been trafficked,

> *When you're a kid how did your mum and dad help you to recover? They didn't put you into a dark... well, hopefully, they didn't put you in a dark room and give you no nice food, and nothing to work for, did they? They gave you a little tray, with biscuits and treats and you'd be in a warm place and...and people will be showing that they outwardly cared. That puts you a step towards getting better.*
>
> Jo

> **In the image of God...**
>
> The Christian understanding of human nature begins with the idea that humans are created "in the image of God", described in the Bible in Genesis 1.26-27. What does this mean? Interpretations naturally differ but we might highlight three elements. First, that we are created: we do not make ourselves, but are embodied, dependent on something else (God) for our existence and flourishing, and connected and interdependent with other creatures. Second, that each person a special dignity. As human beings made in God's image, we are each intended for creativity, productivity, generosity, and love. Third, we are relational: made by a God who is a Trinity of love, and for relationship with him and one another, without which we cannot flourish. Where women are unable to fulfil this potential because of the things that have happened to them, seeing them in God's image therefore implies an understanding that they are not defined by their negative experiences, but have an inherent dignity to be honoured – and a wonderful potential to be released.

Meeting women: In the image of God

Staff and volunteers describe the women they support as cherished individuals loved by God. They meet women "in the image of God". In doing so they meet women as equals, and as individuals who deserve care and respect. Consistently throughout the interviews, staff and volunteers talk about the privilege that was being able to meet and form working relationships with women who access the support of their organisation.

> *The values that really stick out to me...one of the biggest ones I think is valuing the individual and valuing people in their God-given image, you know, [valuing] people's like, they're uniquely made in the image of God, and because of that, they have insurmountable worth. And...one person's worth is never higher than the other. And so, with that comes, kind of, an equality of care.*
>
> Margaret

> *Knowing that the women we support are loved and cared for by God. And that they are precious individual creations, who... God has made for a much better life, a much better purpose than what they are existing in. And if Jesus came for us to have life and have it in abundance...That is not what I see in the lives of the women we work with, so I know God has so much more for them.*
>
> Lydia

Social care is undertaken within and through relationships[11] and it is imperative the impact of trauma experienced by women is understood when developing and delivering helping services.

We know that women have a clear preference for how they are met by staff in helping services, and when this doesn't happen, they will leave the service and not return – putting them at further risk of harm and exploitation.[12] Women often approach helping services for support when they are in a state of distress, but unsure if they will get the help they need. This fact places even greater importance on the way women are heard, met, and listened to.

Having a starting point where women are met in the image of God, and all that this implies for the staff and volunteers, is a powerful dynamic, creating much of what we already know is helpful to develop trusting support relationships. As McClusky explains,

> *Care seekers read faces and respond to what they see there, just as we read other people's faces in response to their expressions.*[13]

When care seekers and care givers meet, it is an interaction, rather than a one-way communication of help given to someone in need.[14] Meeting as equals is imperative.

Staff and volunteers describe it as a privilege to work alongside women. They understand how hard it is for women to trust people to help. The individual value and strength of each woman is recognised and respected.

> *I see it as a real privilege that women who've been so let down, damaged by many people allow you into their lives...They're amazing people, amazing women, just like most women are when you really get to know somebody.*
>
> Alice

> *They're putting their trust in you, which is, you know, why would they do that? They're very brave, they've already been hurt. And it is a privilege to be able to say, okay, this is a safe space that I will make for you.*
>
> Frances

In the previous section we considered the frequent invisibility of women (pp. 67-69). There was a sense here that seeing women in the image of God made them and their lived experiences more visible. The women behind the 'problems' were seen, and so was the complexity of the things that happened to them.

The extra mile: forming and maintaining relationships

There was frequent reference to "going the extra mile" in the interviews, and this application of scripture (Matthew 5.41) to the work of the charity underpins some of the essential elements of practice which are known to be helpful and supportive for women.

> ...Don't just go one mile... Go another mile with a person in need so you know...that's where it comes from...you give wholeheartedly to what you do.
>
> Eva

> ...faith is foremost, because it's just in everything that we do. And I think it's also the reason why we go the extra mile. So for me...it's more than...just a job...I just feel like faith is in everything that we do, in how we interact with the women in what we provide...and going the extra mile. So we don't stop, we keep going...
>
> Tola

> ❝
>
> **Megan talks about how grateful she is that they are fully-funded by their Church and outlines how this has direct implications for the relationships they can form with women.**

In response to a question about how women might know that they (the staff) genuinely cared, Lydia comments,

> Because of the consistency, and sometimes it is dogged determination as well...to build and maintain that relationship.

> So they've built up the relationships sort of slowly and slowly...when I started...there was a few people that used to come, take the goodie bags and then they'd be off...I think even then I remember thinking well...this is a bit cheeky...but then by month six, seven and eight, you saw them stop a bit more and they'd

be like, oh how are you? And how are you? And would stop...and then...few weeks ago just a full-blown conversation with someone that just used to take stuff off us and go...

Jackie

Jackie reflects on this commitment to "go the extra mile" and compares her current role to a previous job. She notes that there is more patience for women in her current role,

...mostly, by week three, we'd write them off and say okay they didn't engage and then you might start writing stuff to the social worker, no not engaging in...not doing this or that, and I suppose it makes them (women) pull away even more.

Having the time and commitment to wait until women are ready to trust staff to help is essential.[15] We know that women test staff and check out if they can be trusted to help.[16] This takes time and can be through small acts like receiving a cup of coffee, a staff member making a phone call, or simply just doing what they said they were going to do. Yet time is often limited through service contract obligations, funding and finite resources.

Repeatedly, this long-term reliable, consistent, and non-judgemental support was the key resource that the charities involved in this study appeared to provide to women. This reflects much of the literature, outlining how FBOs are more likely to favour unconditional approaches of providing support.[17]

Megan talks about how grateful she is that they are fully-funded by their Church and outlines how this has direct implications for the relationships they can form with women and with staff at other organisations, which are essential to provide effective support.

Developing and maintaining support relationships with women is described as one of high points in their work. This is what staff and volunteers enjoy most about their role: being able to provide support for other women and being trusted to do so.

> **Prayer seems to provide a way of reflecting on the things that happen in the course of their work, a gift that could be given to the women they meet and to each other.**

I'm not, I'm just the helper, I'm just the person holding the map, but they choose the route...(this concept) just gave me a new way in terms of engaging, and on a ...more of an empathy level and more of like, a genuine friendship level.

Margaret

But it isn't just knowing that relationships are good for women, making relationships with women is beneficial for the staff and volunteers.

I've really enjoyed the relational side of just knowing that you've made a difference and knowing...you've kind of bought a bit of warmth and a bit of friendship.

Sarah

However, there is an impact on staff. Eva comments that by consistently going the extra mile for women, she believes that,

...we do that sometimes to our own detriment...

Staff and volunteers bear the burden of witnessing the harm and abuse women experience, the poor support sometimes offered by other organisations, and wider social injustice. Whilst it may be a privilege to work with women, it is not without an impact on those that provide the help and support. Throughout interviews staff and volunteers voice frustrations about local and national policy that continues to let women down and cause further harm, the way that 'help' is offered to women, and the limitations of what charities could reasonably do.

Individuals' faith and the collective faith of organisations, seems to provide a way of responding to these aspects of supporting others that at times can leave staff and volunteers with feelings of frustration, disappointment, exhaustion, and concern. Throughout the interviews there is frequent reference to prayer, including how individuals 'leant into it' for strength and how it brought teams together. The application of prayer in practice is explored further below.

Prayer: A gift, reflection, and unity

We start each morning, as a team with God in prayer...ask for prayer requests for the day, and support each other...and during the day, whatever the situation we feel is necessary, we will stop and pray.

Eva

We didn't ask overtly about prayer in the interviews with staff and volunteers, but it is the most mentioned topic of the interviews. Prayer seems to provide a way of reflecting on the things that happen in the course of their work, a gift that could be given to the women they meet and to each other. It also appears to provide a way of unifying teams with a collective space to share concerns and hopes while acknowledging that things are difficult.

As discussed earlier, the diversity of the Christian charities and the beliefs of staff and volunteers vary. About two thirds of the organisations say that they pray together;

other interviewees refer to personal prayer. There are staff and volunteers who do not mention prayer in the interviews, and/or are not of faith, so whilst this is a popular area of discussion, it is important to note that it is not universal. Our aim is not to compare those who pray with those who did not.

A gift to give

We know that women look for aspects of caring amongst staff and volunteers in their body language, in the way that they do things, and in the way that they talk. But beyond these actions there is little that staff and volunteers can say that clearly states how much they care for the women they support. Offering, or asking, to pray for someone or something can be an overt expression of saying that the person is cared for. It is a way of saying that we have witnessed your situation and circumstances, we understand they are difficult, and we would like to express our love and care for you.

Prayer is a gift that staff and volunteers can give to women; they are expressing and sharing their beliefs, and within it telling women how much they do care for them.

It is about sharing our beliefs within the work, and if appropriate, we will, we would say that to the women, and we would ask them, make it known that we pray, they know that we pray each morning...and they can come and ask for prayer if they want to, we can ask them, if they want us to pray for them in a particular situation, we can tell them that we are praying, we will be praying for them, if they're in court, if they're, you know, going through a difficult time. When they leave refuge, when they leave community, they know that we will be there.

Eva

...at the end of our interactions, we always say to people, is there...something we can pray for you...it's very much an

invitation that, you know, they're free to go, oh, no...the majority of time people will go, oh, yeah, can you pray for, you know, whatever...

Sarah

Through offering to pray for women, staff and volunteers are acknowledging and recognising that something is hard for individuals. This lends a human element, in contrast to elements of care provision which at times can feel very procedural and transactional. It leans more to the relational approaches to care.

> **It is interesting to compare the way staff and volunteers describe the act of prayer to a reflective cycle.**

One time, she's telling us about her son, he was in prison. And, and it was really difficult. And she's saying in a very kind of like dispassionate way. And at the end of it was, you know, I said something like, that, that's really hard. Could we pray for you? And she said, oh, yeah, okay. We just started praying for her. And she just started crying...it's like, when you pray for somebody... it kind of slips past all their barriers, and just melts all their defences...there is there's something really powerful about offering to pray for somebody.

Sarah

We're not an organisation to scream about our faith, but we are always willing to pray for people and it's surprising how keen they are to be prayed for...would you like me to pray for you and almost invariably they say of yes please... tell me somebody who doesn't cry out to God, when they're in a desperate situation.

Lydia

As reflective practice

There are many times when practitioners are left with feelings of helplessness or frustration; reflective practice, peer support, and supervision are all considered essential tools to manage the impact of this.[18] Reflective practice[19] underpins social work and social care and is embedded as a learning tool in multiple other professions. The Health and Care Professions Council write that, "creating the space to reflect on your practice, by yourself, with a colleague or as part of a group, can help you to deal with high levels of pressure and share lessons learned to strengthen the important bonds within and across teams."[20] With this in mind, it is interesting to compare the way staff and volunteers describe the act of prayer to a reflective cycle.

We heard from several staff and volunteers how praying offers additional strength. As Margaret explains,

I was kind of reminded...I don't have to depend on myself. I can also...I can lean into God for strength and help.

Margaret

Margaret goes on to illustrate her point with an example,

I was completely overwhelmed....And I just sat there and was like, God, I can't deal with this person anymore...every time she (service user) called I'd get a little like panic attack, because I had no idea who was going to be on the other side of the line, you know whether it's going to be someone super happy, or someone just yelling at me. And then God just asked me, he's like, you haven't prayed about it...why haven't you? Why haven't you like asked me about it? And I was like, right? Why don't I ask you about it? And I just sat there, and I just prayed over her and prayed over the situation.

Below is an image of Gibb's[21] reflective cycle (as one example of many reflective models and tools that have been developed), and we can start to see some overlaps with staff and volunteers' descriptions of prayer in their work, such as establishing that things are difficult and how the member of staff may be feeling about the situation, sharing things that went or didn't go well, talking about things that were hard, as a way of asking for help from others and from God, and exploring what else could be done or what could be done differently in the future.

Figure 1. Gibbs Reflective framework[22]

Whilst we are not comparing the effectiveness of reflective practice and prayer, it is evident that staff and volunteers use prayer as a place to pause and reflect, and as a result gather strength in their emotional labour.

Prayer is part of staff and volunteers' daily work. It seems to provide a place to acknowledge that things are difficult, share problems and feelings of responsibility, and seek support.

Lydia and Eva explain the way prayer gives strength in their work. Lydia also questions how staff in other organisations can do this work without God.

> ...it isn't my full responsibility, it's God's responsibility and I can take it to him...so this is where you draw the strength from your faith...is knowing that...however hidden those things are from other people, that God sees it all, and he cares. He loves those women so much more than I ever can...the fact that we can come together and pray is, you know, massive...
>
> Lydia

> ...being with my colleagues and being able to pray and read the word with them on a daily basis. Before we start our work, during our work - we can stop and say 'you know what, Lord, we don't know what we're going to do here, just help us or you know, give us honesty in this situation'.
>
> Eva

Bringing unity

Prayer is egalitarian: it can be done anywhere and be led by anyone, with other people or on one's own. It doesn't have to wait until a fixed time in the calendar or happen once a month at a supervision appointment.

Chloe explains how the act of prayer brought unity to the team. Chloe has a Muslim faith and talks about the overlap between Christian and Muslim values, and how much she appreciates working in a Christian organisation. She feels that by working at a faith-based organisation, her own faith is better understood and respected,

> ...it feels like a unity, like there's a unit in the room. Even though we are praying to different...I wouldn't even say different Gods, they just got a different like belief. It...it gives me a sense of belonging. And I know that if I had any prayer needs, they'd be able to pray for me and vice versa. I'm praying for them. So it's just a really nice atmosphere and team to work with.

Chloe goes on to explain how starting the day in prayer makes her more present in her work, as if it acted as a transition from her life outside of work to her role supporting women and their children at the refuge.

> ...when I came here...and they do it every morning... it was quite refreshing to me that, oh okay, I can take this time out and you know, pray to my God...it's really nice.... Well, it makes me more, I'd say positive. So, if I'm going through, let's say you have down days, everyone has down days, but in the morning, when they do that prayer, it gives you that bit of uplift of my spiritual lift that you need. So...when you go inside with the children, it just gives you that extra oomph...

Whilst prayer is not discussed by all interviewees, and a number of the staff and volunteers involved do not identify as having a faith, we have discussed here how it brought people together. Prayer appears to be connecting and unifying. It acts as a gift to women, showing that they care and understand things are difficult. Interviewees also talk about charity trustees praying for teams, and churches praying for the charities undertaking work in their communities and the women they supported. It connects the beneficiaries of the charity to its supporters.

There is much talk about the value of reflective practice in social care and beyond (policing, education and business management, amongst others), but frequently there are various time, workload and supervisory limitations which impinge on its actual use in practice. In prayer, staff pause, reflect, share, and listen with frequency. It is integrated with staff and volunteers' way of being and work. Prayer gives a place to acknowledge that the work they are doing is hard and enables people to ask questions and get support. It is accessible, available, and can be done in the moment, or as part of regular meetings. It is something to 'lean into' for strength.

Prayer can therefore be one form of resource. The following section explores broader ideas of resources and how they inform the support organisations provide.

> And, you know that the little bits that we can do, so many agencies can't do. But those little bits that sometimes seem insignificant, ... [are the] things that have made them succeed.

Resources: tensions and opportunities

The resources an organisation can call upon shape the possibilities for action. Equally how these resources are used will reflect the organisation's ethos. Participants were keen to reflect on how they use the resources available to them, and how they deal with some of the tensions and conflicting priorities encountered.

Filling the gaps

Staff comment often on the role their organisations can play in filling the gaps left by and between statutory agencies. This reflects a common view within literature that FBOs' provision supplements the deficiencies of state welfare support.[23] As noted in earlier sections, women seldom receive the kind of support necessary to manage the severe and multiple disadvantage they experience. Staff identify different types of support they can offer. Kate speaks of the value of giving small gifts,

> ...they're always very grateful for the bags, they – they seem to like, you know, the gifts side of things. There's always as I say, a card in there to, you know, give them some support and tell them they're precious...
>
> Kate

This kind of aid is outside the scope of most agencies, which tend to focus more on basic, risk-led provision. Gift-giving is an important way of establishing personal relationships,[24] with feasible – useful and convenient – gifts bringing the most closeness. The gifts reflect the impulse to connect and include through offering something beyond a statutory service.

> **Some participants report that the ways in which their organisations are funded mean they are able to have greater security of resource.**

At other times, a gap may be filled with persistence and a longer-term view of support.

> *...just not giving up because they ain't answered the phone to you for two weeks. And then - and then to see the difference in them further along the line.*
>
> Alice

This approach contrasts with that taken by more mainstream agencies, which might close a case due to 'failure to engage'. Secular services have faced the charge of treating people as cases.[25] The staff in this study took the stance of holistic positive regard. This attitude to care and support is itself a resource, as the following quote from Sarah illustrates,

> *And we also offer like, you know, practical stuff, so somebody needs a lift or somebody to go to a meeting or you know...to church.... But the primary, the primary thing is just being ... with somebody in that moment, kind of listening and caring, and helping and, you know, whatever we can bring in that moment and, and trying to show God's love in that moment to that person.*

Two distinctive things about care stand out from this comment. First, there is the recognition that providing a service alone is often not enough: women may have to be supported to use the support. Second, providing that support is in itself an opportunity to connect. The resources for caring are thus not simply the service itself, but the willingness to be part of that process and to share the regard which stems from faith. This reduces the likelihood of women feeling like they are somehow 'other' and reflects a spirit of hospitality and generosity as a distinctive underpinning for social action.[26]

The things that filled these gaps are often called 'the little things' by staff, but it is clear that they feel they have a much bigger impact.

And, you know that the little bits that we can do, so many agencies can't do. But those little bits that sometimes seem insignificant, ... [are the] things that have made them succeed.
Alice

I know that there are times when in your life, or there'd be times in my life, when sometimes it's quite a small thing that somebody has said or done. That's made a massive difference.
Lydia

Continuity and trust

Some participants report that the ways in which their organisations are funded mean they are able to have greater security of resource. This provides support for staff and removes a source of anxiety. Megan comments,

I am really grateful that [organisation] fully funds us because I'm not scrambling around or stressing out about funding.

This sense of security facilitates sustainable planning, which translates into continuity of provision and the opportunity to form longer-term relationships with women. Megan goes on to describe how damaging it can be when commissioning policies result in short-termism,

I did write actually...a couple of years ago, there was government report to you know, why what works, what doesn't work, and I was like, stop going for the cheapest bid. Because you lose all of the expert knowledge... you lose all our relationship. And the women have to start all over again. And that's not okay.

The lack of long-term and appropriate support for women experiencing severe and multiple disadvantage has long been emphasised by campaigning organisations.[27] Megan's comments highlight that developing a relationship over time can be central in providing effective support to women. When organisations can access reliable funding, there is more scope for continuity of care, which in turn supports a growth in trust. Often FBOs are seen by those who use them as inherently more trustworthy than state bureaucratic services.[28]

Organisations in this research are able to rely on support from within their faith communities, which is common amongst FBOs.[29] This sometimes gives scope for creative approaches to problems, such as fundraising to support specific capital projects and drawing on networks. Jo described being able to raise money to build a much-needed space for her service.

Of course, inevitably there are participants who report resource constraints, which affect the depth of service they can offer. Some organisations are very dependent on individuals volunteering, hence there are difficulties when they are unavailable. Kate makes monthly visits within her service, so missing a day leads to long gaps,

> **Inevitably there are participants who report resource constraints, which affect the depth of service they can offer.**

I couldn't go this last Wednesday because I had to go to a funeral. So I haven't been for a little while, which is just frustrating with [it only] being once a month, but so yeah, and so it's just, it's a very slow process.

Kate

Fighting for women or fighting for justice?

One tension which participants report is whether their resources should be deployed to serve women directly or used to campaign for broader social change. Staff inevitably become acutely aware of the injustices which women experienced. Although in some respects, access to independent resources gives FBOs more freedom to speak out, focusing on the women more than wider issues can also be seen as diplomatic and a way of forging relationships with other agencies.

> ...we tend to keep a low profile to try and do what we do for the women well... but I think, and we try to stay out of politics and things because we're about the women, as always, and we're trying, we try to work with different agencies so that we've got good connections.
>
> Alice

Staff sometimes take an apolitical stance in order to help themselves centre on the women as individuals. However, this stance can also leave staff feeling powerless to effect change. Lydia's comments express this dilemma:

> Where do you put... where do you put your, your time? Do you put your time into screaming and raising awareness? Or do you put your time in - that a woman who's sofa surfing, got horrendous medical needs, struggling to keep in drug treatment and also hasn't got anywhere to live herself?
>
> Lydia

There is no uniform stance amongst FBOs in general in relation to this dilemma. Some actively campaign for social justice,[30] whilst others remain neutral. It is evident that this represents a source of ethical challenge for staff, and it is difficult for them not to feel pulled in different directions. This can be a source of stress when a key concern is to act with care and compassion.

Staff also encounter significant problems when trying to support women to use other services which are poorly designed or inappropriate for their needs. Megan illustrates these challenges:

> *So the current...rough sleeping guidance, is that they have to be seen bedded down at night. I can, you know, hear how that doesn't.... And for street sex workers who might be homeless... they're not going to be able to access your service... because they're.... working during the night. And so when I put a street link application in for someone who is sleeping in a toilet during the day, they're like, we can't access those.*
>
> Megan

Therefore, even when staff focus on supporting individual women, they might find themselves liaising with other agencies to try to educate or promote change in service delivery. It has been argued that FBOs, particularly in sectors such as homelessness services, are not as interventionist as secular agencies, meaning they are less focused on trying to promote behaviour change amongst the people with whom they work.[31] In some respects, staff in this study seem to be more focused on changing and influencing the nature and appropriateness of mainstream provision rather than changing the behaviour of the women who rely upon it.

1 Hodges and Burch, 'Multiple and Intersecting Experiences of Women in Prostitution...'

2 Neale and Hodges, '"My Head Was Like a Washing Machine on Spin..."'; McCluskey, *To Be Met as a Person*.

3 Ministry of Justice, 'A Whole System Approach for Female Offenders - Emerging evidence', 2018, p. 14 *https://assets.publishing.service.gov.uk/government/uploads/system/uploads/attachment_data/file/719771/guide-to-whole-system-approach.pdf*

4 Neale and Hodges, '"My Head Was Like a Washing Machine on Spin..."'

5 Young, Boyd, and Hubbell, 'Prostitution, Drug Use, and Coping...' (op. cit. Part One); Bindel et al., *Breaking down the Barriers...* (op. cit. Part One)

6 Joanne Bretherton and Nicholas Pleace, *Women's Homelessness in Camden: Improving Data, Strategy, and Outcomes* (York & London: University of York & SHP, 2021). PDF available at: *www.shp.org.uk/Handlers/Download.ashx?IDMF=5fee2c27-c387-4a68-b574-8d00a6ce7e76*; Single Homeless Project, 'Fulfilling Lives in Islington and Camden', 2021, *www.shp.org.uk/fulfillinglives*; Harris and Hodges, 'Responding to Complexity...'; Making Every Adult Matter et al., MEAM Approach, 2018, meam.org.uk/; Bretherton and Pleace, *Women and Rough Sleeping...* (op. cit. Part One); Ministry of Justice, 'A Whole System Approach...'; Harris, *Response to Complexity* (R2C): Final Evaluation.

7 Harris and Hodges, 'Responding to Complexity...'

8 Bretherton and Pleace, *Women's Homelessness in Camden...*

9 Hodges, *An Exploration of Decision Making...*

10 Hodges, *An Exploration of Decision Making...*

11 Gillian Ruch, 'Relationship-based practice and reflective practice: holistic approaches to contemporary child care social work', *Child and Family Social Work* Vol 10, No. 2 (May 2005), p. 111–123. *doi.org/10.1111/j.1365-2206.2005.00359.x*

12 Hodges, *An Exploration of Decision Making...*

13 McCluskey, *To Be Met as a Person...* p.248

14 McCluskey, *To Be Met as a Person...*

15 Hodges, *An Exploration of Decision Making...*

16 Hodges, *An Exploration of Decision Making...*

17 Johnsen, 'Where's the "Faith" in "Faith-Based" Organisations?...'; Bode, 'Disorganized welfare mixes...'

18 Gary Rolfe and Dawn Freshwater, *Critical Reflection In Practice: Generating Knowledge for Care*, Second edition (Oxford: Macmillan Education, 2011);

Jan Fook and Fiona Gardner, *Practising critical reflection: a resource handbook*, (London: Open University Press, 2007); Peter John Hawkins and Robin Shohet, *Supervision in the Helping Professions*, (London: Open University Press, 2007); Sue Thompson and Neil Thompson, *The Critically Reflective Practitioner* (Basingstoke: Palgrave Macmillan, 2008); Ming-sum Tsui, *Social Work Supervision: Contexts and Concepts,* (Thousand Oaks, California: SAGE Publications, 2005).

19 Reflective practice in its simplest form is a way to think about what is happening in your work, reflect on what can be learnt, consider and analyse its impact, and begin to think about a plan of action and what you might do differently next time.

20 Health and Care Professions Council, 'Reflective Practice', 2021, *www.hcpc-uk.org/standards/meeting-our-standards/reflective-practice/*

21 Graham Gibbs, *Learning by Doing: A Guide to Teaching and Learning Methods*, (Oxford: Oxford Polytechnic, 1988).

22 Gibbs, *Learning by Doing…*

23 Pennington, *The Church and Social Cohesion…*; Spencer, *Doing Good…*; Teuta Vodo, 'Faith-Based Organisations: The Role of Christian Organizations to Social Cohesion in EU Member States' (European Christian Political Movement., 2016). PDF available at: *https://ecpm.info/FBOs-Paper.pdf*

24 Soyon Rim, Kate Min and Peggy Liu, 'The Gift of Psychological Closeness: How Feasible Versus Desirable Gifts Reduce Psychological Distance to the Giver', in *Personality and Social Psychology Bulletin*, Vol 45, No. 3 (2019), *doi/10.1177/0146167218784899*

25 Beth R. Crisp, 'Challenges to Organizational Spirituality as a Consequence of State Funding', *Journal for the Study of Spirituality* Vol 5, No. 1 (May 2015), p. 47–59, *doi.org/10.1179/2044024315Z.00000000040*

26 Rich, *Growing Good…*

27 Agenda, 'Agenda Briefing: Women facing multiple disadvantage', 2019, *https://weareagenda.org/wp-content/uploads/2019/01/Multiple-disadvantage-Jan-2019-1.pdf*

28 Paul Oslington, 'Sacred and secular in Australian social services', Pacifica: Australasian Theological Studies Vol 28, No. 1 (February 2015), p. 79–93, *doi.org/10.1177/1030570X15619782*

29 Johnsen, 'Where's the "Faith" in "Faith-Based" Organisations?…'

30 Paul Cloke, Sam Thomas, and Andrew Williams, 'Faith in Action: Faith-Based Organizations, Welfare and Politics in the Contemporary City', in Paul Cloke, Justin Beaumont, and Andrew Williams (ed), *Working Faith: Faith-Based Organizations and Urban Social Justice*, (Milton Keynes: Paternoster, 2013).

31 Johnsen, 'Where's the "Faith" in "Faith-Based" Organisations?…'

Conclusion

This research has been undertaken during the COVID-19 pandemic, when the role of FBOs and communities has been increasingly recognised.[1] In the past two years, FBOs have been seen as adding value to the limited resources and capacity of local statutory services. Mainstream forms of social support have struggled to cope with the rapidly changing context in which access to services has been disrupted and demand for aid has risen massively. There are ongoing discussions taking place about the way faith communities do this work, and how their offer is integrated into local provision.[2] Therefore, looking at how the Christian charities involved in this study talk about the support they offer, their experiences of providing it, how their faith is evident and whether this constitutes a distinctive approach, is timely.

The support FBOs can offer is influenced by access to resources and how they choose to use them. FBOs tend to have access to longer term funding through their supporters and churches, which reduces or supplements any reliance on statutory funding. This often means that they will have long histories in areas where they work, having been a consistent provider of care over years, building up long term relationships with service users and other providers. We heard from staff and volunteers about how they saw other provision come and go, as short-term funding came to an end and new projects were commissioned. The opportunity to build reliable, sustainable provision is important for FBOs.

FBOs also prefer to provide unconditional as well as longer-term support (see p. 51), which is arguably more helpful to women experiencing multiple and severe disadvantage. In this study, we heard about a range of work carried out by the Christian charities involved; it was variable and often fell outside the types of support that would be commissioned as part of statutory responses. The focus on relational and unconditional practice, sometimes without detailed knowledge of the 'problem' or the outcomes they were seeking to achieve – enables a flexibility to provide support in a way that is responsive to women.

Visibility

What was striking about the charities' work was that it was largely invisible, as were the women helped by this work. Some of the charities involved had little recognition from local statutory services and commissioners, and there seemed to be a lack of knowledge or concern about the extent of the extreme disadvantage women experienced.[3] There is much written about the invisibility of women and their experiences, but ignorance continues about the impact of intersecting oppressions and how this affects help-seeking and navigating the complex world and systems of support services. There is a resistance to seeing women as whole humans rather than a long list of problems to be neatly resolved by individual responses.

When we turn to the experiences of staff and volunteers offering support, what stood out was the way they saw and valued the women with whom they worked. Whilst this may not be unique to staff and volunteers in FBOs, the participants in this study witnessed the pain and the distress women experienced. They understood the complexity of situations and the fact that there were no easy one-stop solutions, working hard to establish trusting relationships as a priority. They saw the injustice and barriers that were preventing women who had extensive histories of trauma from accessing the support they needed. Staff and volunteers worked tirelessly to navigate systems to help women access the support they needed. It is not unique for staff and volunteers at FBOs to witness the pain and distress women experience; rather it is interesting to hear from the participants in this study how their faith and personal values informed their work.

The flexibility of the parameters of staff and volunteers' roles, mostly resulting from resourcing (financial or volunteering), gave them the opportunity to do this in a way some short-term funded/outcome-focused services based on policy demands cannot. The experiences and knowledge of the staff working at these FBOs should be heard. There is much to be learnt in what they have witnessed, and there are many obvious ideas for system change that would significantly benefit the women they support.

> **The focus on relational and unconditional practice, sometimes without detailed knowledge of the 'problem' or the outcomes they were seeking to achieve, enables a flexibility to provide support in a way that is responsive .**

Notably, all the staff and volunteers to whom we spoke were women (many of the services had requirements for female staff under Equalities Act provision). Supporting extremely disadvantaged women, hearing about the suffering they have gone through, and continuing to witness the disadvantage they could experience in the wider systems which are meant to help them, is not easy. This is hard work, and it is being done quietly. Invisible women are supported by invisible staff.

Staff need to be recognised as having this value and insight, but it is also important to acknowledge and respond to the pull on their focus in terms of where they put their energies and resources. We heard how difficult it was for them to work in a space where the fight for justice often seemed at odds with their duty to women, leaving staff uncertain where to focus resources. If this experience goes unheard, it becomes another way that women's experiences remain invisible.

Faith in practice

We saw numerous respects in which the faith of staff and volunteers was evident. They talked of its influence on what they do and how they do it. Staff and volunteers brought faith to their work in distinctive ways, and it underpinned how they met women and provided support. Faith was infused into practice. Meeting women in the image of God further enforced the idea of how the women they supported were equals who deserved better. Going the extra mile informed their consistency and commitment. Faith brought visibility and compassion.

Faith also seemed to be of value to the staff and volunteers as they undertook this difficult yet essential labour. Prayer was spoken of as a hugely valuable asset, bringing comfort and unity. It had much in common with secular notions of reflective practice but had a greater capacity to offer comfort to those who practised it. The relationships that staff and volunteers built with women were the highlight of their work. But seeing women consistently let down, or being abused/exploited again, or going back to harmful patterns of behaviour, was inevitably hard. Faith and prayer were ways in which staff and volunteers could support themselves and each other in terms of their own well-being in the face of such challenges.

The aim of this research was not to compare Christian charities and secular organisations. Numerous studies have identified that the boundaries between these sectors are blurred. However, we found elements of care amongst these six Christian charities that were distinctive if not unique. These came through in different ways across the range of organisations in the study. As earlier noted, "faith is not a predictor of how an agency operates and its interactions with clients."[4]

What stood out in this study was the way that faith allowed different groups of women to relate, connect and become visible to one another. Faith was part of the motivation of staff and volunteers, providing support to women in often desperate circumstances. Faith enabled them to experience a sense of unity within their organisations and to work with women from a position of equal value.

Meeting women, valuing women

It is evident that there are things that can be learnt from the way these six Christian charities support women experiencing severe and multiple disadvantage. The first is their relational approach to practice, understanding as much as possible about the intersecting lived experiences of women, the complexity this creates and the barriers to seeking help and support. They meet women with this knowledge, working to ensure that they can create environments of trust and safety.

Building trusting relationships takes time and patience. This time frequently expands beyond the limits of when many other services would provide support. The commitment to be present for women, even if they are unable (for whatever reason) to attend or make use of the support available. This is less about women being 'motivated to attend' or 'not engaging', and more about choosing to access support and help on their terms and in a way that feels safe to them.

Faith and personal beliefs informed the way staff and volunteers met women. Whilst many organisations will have values of equality, empowerment, non-judgemental and anti-oppressive practice, it appeared that practitioners' faith made this translatable to their practice. With faith informing their personal values, service beneficiaries are considered equals and every aspect of service delivery begins from this point.

Whilst prayer is not something all individuals and organisations may be able or want to bring into their practice, there is something to be learnt from staff making time to pause and reflect. Pausing and reflecting can occur at organised times, but also as the need arises. Reflective practice provides a clear model to do some of this, but aspects of comfort found in prayer are less available. Leaning into God for strength is hard to replicate, but there are aspects of this that would benefit from being explored further.

Christian charities are part of a bigger network and community of support. The nature of what they do is shared within the wider faith communities and in return they receive support, often through prayer and resources (financial, volunteering and donations such as food, clothes etc). If more is to be done to make invisible women visible and valued, then arguably there is a network of faith communities which are well placed to bring attention to the injustice, the care needed, and the care provided.

1 All Party Parliamentary Group for Faith and Society, 'Keeping the Faith - Partnerships between faith groups and local authorities during and beyond the pandemic', 2020, *www.faithandsociety.org/wp-content/uploads/APPG_CovidReport_Full_V4.pdf*

2 APPG Faith and Society, 'Keeping the Faith...'; Rich, *Growing Good....*; Pennington, *Social Cohesion and the Church...*

3 Caroline Criado-Perez, *Invisible Women: Exposing Data Bias in a World Designed for Men* (London: Vintage, 2020); Corston, *The Corston Report...*; Ann Oakley, *The Ann Oakley Reader: Gender, Women, and Social Science* (Bristol: Policy Press, 2005); Kimberle Williams Crenshaw, 'Mapping the Margins: Intersectionality, Identity Politics, and Violence against Women of Color (Women of Color at the Center: Selections from the Third National Conference on Women of Color and the Law)', *Stanford Law Review* Vol 43, No. 6 (1991), p. 1241–1299, *doi.org/10.2307/1229039*

4 Smith, Bartkowski, and Grettenberger, 'A Comparative View of the Role and Effect of Faith...', p. 24.

Recommendations

1. **Christian charities need to be recognised and valued locally and nationally for their work in the community, no matter the size or perceived impact of their provision.** They have long-term understanding of the nature of women's experiences in the community and the barriers to/complexity of accessing helping services for women; they hold a history of the things that have happened. They have significant knowledge, understanding and relationships which need to be valued and incorporated in local and national policy, planning and service delivery.

2. **Relational and trauma informed approaches to care are well evidenced, but the application to practice is harder, particularly within restrictive funding scenarios. Much can be learnt from the way the Christian charities involved in this study provided support and incorporated into wider practice.** It is essential that providers of care and support for women understand that complex histories of trauma have significant implications on help-seeking. Helping services must be present for women, when they wanted support, rather than at prescribed times. Women should not be 'discharged' for 'not engaging'. Positive outcomes are relative to each and every woman, they cannot be based on policy derived priorities for behaviour change.

3. **Services and staff need support in challenging the bad practice, unhelpful service provision or oppressive systems that they witness.** Current mechanisms are falling short. This is not only very harmful for women, but also for the staff and volunteers who support them.

4. **Repeatedly it has been evidenced that safe, secure, and supported housing for women is a priority.** There is an opportunity here for FBOs to bring their unconditional approaches to care, long term relationships, and alternative funding and resourcing, to consider how they can develop effective residential support for women.

5. Elements of this research that would benefit from being explored further.

    a. There is **limited research exploring women and FBOs,** in terms of those receiving and providing care, and this should be remedied given the likely proportion in both groups.

    b. Also, it would be useful to investigate further the threads of **connecting reflective practice and prayer** in care provision, and the **impact of 'going the extra mile'** on staff and volunteers.

6. **Women need to be made visible at every level in the community and beyond.** The situation for women experiencing severe and multiple disadvantage is complex. This needs to be witnessed, and action taken to challenge the ongoing failure to adequately respond and support women. There is space here for faith-based organisations who undertake direct work to consider if they want to campaign and lobby for change. It is for each organisation to decide if and how it wants to make visible the invisible. Staff and volunteers would benefit from support when taking social action, or in deciding not to take it, balancing the tensions of supporting women whilst fighting for justice.

Theos – enriching conversations

Theos exists to enrich the conversation about the role of faith in society.

Religion and faith have become key public issues in this century, nationally and globally. As our society grows more religiously diverse, we must grapple with religion as a significant force in public life. All too often, though, opinions in this area are reactionary or ill informed.

We exist to change this

We want to help people move beyond common misconceptions about faith and religion, behind the headlines and beneath the surface. Our rigorous approach gives us the ability to express informed views with confidence and clarity.

As the UK's leading religion and society think tank, we reach millions of people with our ideas. Through our reports, events and media commentary, we influence today's influencers and decision makers. According to *The Economist*, we're "an organisation that demands attention". We believe Christianity can contribute to the common good and that faith, given space in the public square, will help the UK to flourish.

Will you partner with us?

Theos receives no government, corporate or denominational funding. We rely on donations from individuals and organisations to continue our vital work. Please consider signing up as a Theos Friend or Associate or making a one off donation today.

Theos Friends and Students
— Stay up to date with our monthly newsletter

— Receive (free) printed copies of our reports

— Get free tickets to all our events

£75/ year
for Friends

£40/ year
for Students

Theos Associates
— Stay up to date with our monthly newsletter

— Receive (free) printed copies of our reports

— Get free tickets to all our events

— Get invites to private events with the Theos team and other Theos Associates

£375/ year

Sign up on our website:
www.theosthinktank.co.uk/about/support-us